Import

MW00943332

Lotus Sutra - Faith and Practice

by
Ryusho Jeffus

Important Matters:
Lotus Sutra Faith and Practice

By Ryusho Jeffus
Copyright 2017

Myosho-ji, Wonderful Voice Buddhist Temple
611 Vine St.
Syracuse, NY 13203

ISBN-13: 978-1979530811
ISBN-10: 1979530815

Special Acknowledgement

The official name of the book of standards is titled Shutei Nichiren Shu Hoyo Shiki. It is commonly referred to as Shutei Hoyo Shiki or Hoyo Shiki. The English translation is the first complete translation of this entire book consisting of over 500 pages.

We owe a debt of gratitude to the translation and production committee including Venerable Shokai Kanai, Hirai Shonin, Ryuei McCormick Shonin, Ryuoh Faulconer Shonin, and others. All Nichiren Shu benefits greatly from their efforts.

Contents

More Books by Rysuho Jeffus:

Lecture on the Lotus Sutra

Lotus Sutra Practice Guide

Daily Lotus

Incarcerated Lotus

The Magic City

The Physician's Good Medicine

Lotus Path

King Wonderful Adornment

Lire du Sutra du Lotus

Cité Magique

Le Bon Remède du Médecin Habile

Roi Ornement-Merveilleux

Over several months in the Spring of 2017 I gave a series of lectures on some of the important material available to ministers in the Shutei Hoyo Shiki. Due to the importance of the material I felt it necessary to make it more widely available. Many ministers simply do not have the time to present this material especially given the ongoing nature of teaching basics to new Sangha members. Also, there is so much information that needs to be shared it would be a challenge to anyone even if their sole job was simply to teach. Ministers in the United States are not so blessed since in most instances all the administrative tasks, fund raising, conducting services, as well as provide counseling all usually come on top of holding a job to keep a roof over ones head and food on the table.

As a mostly retired minister who mainly hosts an online sangha and who helps Kanjin Shonin with the training of his disciples I have a certain luxury of some freedom to focus on things which I feel are important and make them available to as wide an audience as possible. It doesn't mean I have unlimited time, and even if I did I do not have unlimited energy. So before judging a minister for not providing what I am going to provide you, and before judging what I have chosen please bear in mind that we all do the best we are able. And that holds true for you.

The best you are able to do today may not be the best you were able to do yesterday or could do tomorrow, it is however the best you are able to do now. So it is with everyone.

I leave you with this quote from the Shutei Hoyo Shiki.

The way we are and the state of our mind in any moment is the relationship we experience with the Three Treasures. There is no distinction. We are either constantly bowing, or not bowing but always manifesting our relationship.

Shutei Hoyo Shiki - History and Background

The first publication of this book, which presents the standards and protocols, was accomplished in 1951. The effort to produce this book began much earlier. In response to a wartime government decree, three Nichiren schools – Nichiren Shu, Honmon Shu, and Kempon Hokke Shu – merged into today's Nichiren Shu on April 3, 1941.

Included in the first Shutei Hoyo Shiki were documents and letters providing important background on the motivations for the merger and the creation of this book. It is in the spirit of understanding and clarification that I present a summary of this important information here.

Before becoming a Nichiren Shu priest, I practiced in a different denomination of Nichiren Buddhism, a school that remains separate. That school questions the motivations of the merger and the outcome, believing it to have been a heretical action. What that school never presented was proof of such an interpretation.

Anyone is free to interpret events as they wish, and frequently people do so to better their image or cause. That is the nature of things. If, however, one wishes to engage in scholarly study one must include primary sources such as contemporaneous documents. What is presented in the Shutei Hoyo Shiki are letters of the participants in the events, as well as the words of the priest who was tasked with compiling and eventually publishing this book. This qualifies as a primary source and cannot be ignored, even if one disagrees, a fault of which my previous denomination was guilty.

Special Report of the Three Schools Merging into One - by Nichiken, April 3, 1941

The opening of this report begins with a declaration of the expressions of gratitude of Nichiken by his offering incense and performing a special ceremony before the Great Mandala of the Lotus Sutra which was revealed by Nichiren the founder of Nichiren Buddhism. What follows is most revealing, something which moved me in a deep way.

Nichiken begins by posing the question of why there were divisions into separate lineages when at their core all believe in the Essential Teaching of the Lotus Sutra, and all see themselves as Bodhisattvas who emerged from the ground. This is a question that remains for many today, especially given the rancor of discussions as more Nichiren schools have become active in the United States. In addition, the messy break up of Nichiren Shoshu and Soka Gakkai contributed greatly to the tenor of the dispute. I personally believe it is possible to disagree without disrespect, especially given the fundamental truth to which most schools believe.

Immediately following the death of Nichiren there was an initial split into ten groups that came about because of differences in understanding of the teachings, interpretations of Nichiren's intentions, and the methods of propagation such as whether to use shoju or shakabuku. Over the centuries, the divisions became more pronounced and hardened into different schools. By 1941 each school preserved what it considered right, while defending itself against those who disagreed.

These differences still challenge us as we reflect upon and consider the teaching of itai doshin (different in body and same in mind). Adding to the challenge is the fact that Nichiren Buddhism fundamentally stands for the unification of all Buddhism based upon the supreme teaching of the Lotus Sutra. These teachings are difficult to reconcile with the reality of Nichiren's fractured legacy.

Nichiken acknowledges that the differences did not arise lightly or without careful research and contemplation on the part of many wise priests through the ages. I think this is a gracious statement and one that seeks to build a bridge of respect and cooperation.

Recognizing and honoring the efforts through the ages of men of wisdom and well-meaning intent also calls us to recognize that there were, in some cases, special circumstances that prompted the decisions. For example, before joining Nichiren Shu I was taught that Nichiji Shonin had abandoned the founder's mandate to spread the Lotus Sutra. The truth is that he traveled north in the hope of returning the Lotus Sutra to China. Until recently it was uncertain whether he succeeded. Now archeological discoveries provide evidence that he did accomplish his mission in the Mongolian region of China. The difficulty of reaching China in the 13th century from Hokkaido, the northernmost island of Japan, alone causes me to have great admiration for Nichiji Shonin.

It is a complicated process to unravel the evolution of the differences within each school. Nichiken even points out that the manner of propagation was influenced by persecutions in different locations that may not have been experienced by all disciples.

On October 13, 1922, the emperor conferred the title Rissho Daishi upon Nichiren Shonin, a great honor and a title conveying the importance of Nichiren to Japan. There are, however, those who feel this was on the order of a sacrilege because the emperor and the country had not actually accepted the teaching of Nichiren. I won't discount this view; it is, however, a matter of interpretation. It may be important to you, or you may do as I do and set it aside as something that really doesn't involve me nor impact my belief in the correctness of Nichiren Shonin as taught by Nichiren Shu.

The 1941 unification effort was not the first attempt. Attempts were made in 1902 and 1915. For whatever reasons, the goal was not realized. In the parlance of Buddhism, the time was not yet right. Nichiken suggests that if it were possible to assemble all the various disciples and founders of the different schools they would be pleased with the unification that took place in 1941 and would all make the pilgrimage to visit the founder's grave.

Nichiken states that the beginning of the merger discussions took place in the fall of 1940 and due to the escalation of events outside the realm of religion – World War II – there was an increased pressure to move quickly. Due to this, Nichiken states that there was not enough time to include all the schools.

With the ceremony being performed to report the unification of the three schools Nichiken notes that for the first time in ages the people and Dharma were united and present at the location where Nichiren first moved the Sangha to Mount Minobu. He also includes his invitation that all the schools will one day come to Minobu and bow and pray together at the founder's grave.

The three heads of the schools in attendance were Archbishop Nichiken Mochizuki Kancho of Nichiren Shu, Archbishop Nichikan Imura Kancho of Kempon Hokke Shu, and Archbishop Nichiko Yui Kancho of Honmon Shu.

I'll present the summary of each of the representatives shortly, for now though I'd like to jump forward in time to the 1950s.

"Editorial Notes and Explanations" by Genjo Takahashi, Nov. 25, 1950

Because of the unification of the three schools there needed to be a way for them to join together and perform the ceremonies and to provide a standardized way to instruct new ministers. As you might imagine it was not easy to reconcile all of the differences in each school that had arisen over the centuries. In fact, there were some things much too difficult to tackle, and they were set aside to pursue what was possible.

As if the ironing out of the differences of each school while respecting and understanding them and their importance were not difficult enough, the war imposed greater and greater hardship on the people of Japan. Meetings became increasingly difficult. The roads and rails were either in ruin, taken over by military forces, or the conveyances did not exist or function. Today it is possible to travel from Tokyo

7

to Minobu in a matter of hours with only minor difficulty. During the early 1940s I can only imagine the tremendous burden travelers faced. Remember, the schools were similarly isolated from Minobu.

Included in this portion of the Hoyo Shiki are detailed notes about the decisions made, the reasons for including some things over others, the issues grappled with regarding maintaining old traditional language and usages over more modern conventions. While it is interesting it is really outside of the spirit in which I engaged in writing this book, which was to convey the attitudes of our practice.

"Postscript" by Honshu Nakanishi Director Education Division, Dec. 8, 1950

I'm going to quote the entire first paragraph from Honshu Nakanishi's writing believing I could do no better at expressing his thoughts than he has, important thoughts for us to always maintain as we engage in our own services.

"Ceremonies and protocols are art. Because they are the foundations of noble faith, Nichiren cermonies are a solemn, refined, comprehensive art that is created by our entire body and heart. Anyone who says they are no more than formalized sutra chanting has no idea of their true nature. It is sometimes said that art needs no goal; that art exists for its own sake. Buddhist ceremonies do not exist for proselytizing or teaching. Instead they are supreme expressions of pure, unmitigated devotion to the Three Treasures. Only when this is true can the performer and the observer steep themselves in unobstructed concentrated meditation. From awareness of the true nature of ceremonies, as an unexpected collateral effect, awakening arises."

Kempon Hokke Shu - Archbishop Nichikan Imura Kancho

Noteworthy in Archbishop Nichikan's address is the statement that his lineage founder, Nichiju, did not intend to establish a separate school. He merely wished to spread the teachings and uphold them correctly as he understood them.

I offer here a bit of the history of Kempon Hokke Shu as shared in the Archbishop's address. At the age of 67, Nichiju, already a respected and long-time teacher of the sutras at Mt. Hiei, the center of Tendai Buddhism, developed serious doubts that he could not reconcile and so left his position and returned to his own home mountain temple. It was while there he happened to discover Nichiren's Kaimoku-sho and Nyosetsu Shugyo-sho. After reading and absorbing these two writings, Nichiju's mind was cleared and his doubts removed. At this point he firmly and unequivocally declared Tendai was obsolete and Jikaku's teachings as wicked.

Wishing to act upon his newly found convictions, even at his advanced age, he examined the existing schools of Nichiren Buddhism and felt that they were not acting in accord with the instructions and wishes of Nichiren. He also was dismayed over the fact that the Lotus Sutra, the sutra that seeks to unite all Buddhism, should be so fractured by the arguments of the time. Given these circumstances, he could not see his own efforts joining with any of the existing schools.

Archbishop Nichikan participated in the earlier attempts at unification in 1902 and 1911. It was in 1941, he notes, that voices previously unheard and from all the schools had arisen to call for a unification. Given the circumstances, he says it would have been regrettable if that moment were allowed to slip away. He states it was with great pleasure the other schools decided to merge with Nichiren Shu.

As the heads of the other schools have stated it was his belief that their own founder and all the successive ministers of their lineage would smile favorably on the ceremony and unification.

Contemplation on Entering the Place of Practice

Nyu Dojo Kan

Entering the place of practice can be any space where we dedicate our energy, thoughts, activities to devotion to the Lotus Sutra. It can be a space on a shelf in a small apartment. Also it can be a shared meeting space in someone's home or even a more formal space such as a temple. However for most of us the place of practice we most frequently enter is our own home sacred space. And because it is in our home it is also the one most at risk of being taken for granted or given slighted attention.

The space in our home may be a space we walk by throughout our day in our home. The sacred space may out of necessity be a small portion of a single room used for many functions. This is the reality for many people. Not everyone, in fact few, may be able to afford to live in a place that a dedicated room can serve the single function of a practice space. One is not less significant or less important or meaningful. What makes it so is our attitude to the space.

I have encouraged people who need to have their practice area as part of a multipurpose space to at least try to have the practice or sacred space set off to the side so that it isn't crossed over or passed in front of frequently during the course of everyday usage of the space. So if the sacred space or altar is shared with a computer/entertainment space then

13

have it so those activities are the once which get passed in front of to access the altar and not the other way around. Crossing in front of the altar several times a day to do other things increases the risk that the altar simply becomes part of the scenery. So perhaps if you have such an arrangement consider moving the altar to a far corner so it becomes the focal point for that portion of the room. In such a location it becomes the destination for practice and not a waypoint to doing other things.

Because this section deals with a physical solid structure, a house, building, altar, temple and so forth, the starting reference point is four great elements. Those elements are earth, air, water, and fire, not in any particular order. Everything in the practice space, ourselves included are comprised of these four elements. Because we, the subject, and the space, the object are all composed of the same four elements we are in many respects not separated or different. We ourselves are both the practitioner as well as the place of practice. Our actions towards and in the place of practice are the manifestation of the actions within our own lives.

These four elements have existed in the past, now exist in the present, and will continue to exist into the future even if their physical manifestation is changed. So within the four elements as manifest in this particular time and place in which we are currently practicing in they are connected throughout space and time.

Thinking about what this means can provide a profoundness to something we may not have considered previously. In this moment as we enter or settle in our place of practice we are connected to the infinite past and the infinite future both metaphysically, in our minds and live force, as well as physically in our four elements. As we enter into the practice space whether it is a great hall or the altar on the bookshelf in our tiny apartment we are entering into a much deeper experience than the mere appearance of the altar or room or even the aches of our bones as we take our seat. This space is the space of the entire universe from the past into the future. From this perspective our reciting of the sutra, which we may at times feel insignificant or tiny is expansive enough to fill the entire universe. No longer are you seated in front of a cardboard box with a piece of paper hanging in front of you. You have entered into the great and infinite universe as told by the Buddha in the Sutras.

This practice space is not simply a place of practice it is the place of practice.

The Shute Hoyo Shiki says:

> *"When the practitioner enters into the place of practice he [she] should contemplate the following: Now this place of practice is composed of the four great elements. These four great elements pervade the ten directions in the past, present, and future.[1]"*

In our present existence it isn't possible for us to see deep into the molecular structure of all that exists along side of us. We are not naturally endowed with electron microscopic eyesight. Yet even though imperceptible everything around and within us is composed of the elements of earth, wind, water, and fire from a Buddhist perspective. And just as all the things manifest around us are composed of these elements so too are our very own bodies.

---

1 Shute Hoyo Shiki - Udana-in Nichiki - page 389

We may tend to view things in terms of this and that, self and other, in fact there is no distiction when viewed from the perspective of Buddhism. The sepperation is merely an illusion, one that can at times serve us well or serve us poorly. When we ignore or fail to appreciate the things around us we are failing to appreciate the very essence of our own lives, or worse perhaps we may consider ouselves supperior and even removed from the things in our environment. The attitudes we hold about our environment are ultimately reflected in our attitudes about self.

How we treat our home and our practice space whether it be in our home or in a great temple is not seperable from how we fundamentally treat our lives. It is only an illusion or a fairy tale that one can slight or treat casually the practice space and then say they treat their own lives with reverence. From the truth of oneness of subject and object it isn't possible to treat the object one way and then say the subject is treated another way. The reverse is also true. Treating the object or place of practice with reverence is not possible if one does not truly treat one's own life as equally reverential.

All of this is also influenced by the results of past causes. Our past causes manifesting in the present are the ground upon which we need to make changes. In the past one may have ignored the place of practice, or taken it for granted. That space then becomes harder to change into a place of reverence and respect. We have set in motion the nature of our behavior and the current manifestations are the hurdles we will need to overcome in order to significantly make necessary changes in order to have future manifestations be altered.

In the Lotus Sutra before the Buddha elevates the congregation to enable everyone to see Many Treasures Buddha he first purifies the land. The new space is not large enough so he brings in more realms from the universe. These too he purifies. This continues until he finally has enough space for all beings. As we approach our practice space regardless of its location we have a choice in how we do this.

We can simply enter, giving no thought to purification and expansion. This limits us and inhibits a profound and infinite connection to the Dharma of the Lotus Sutra, the Dharma for the infinite universe, the Dharma for time past, present, and future. It is as if we only are interested in purifying and making space for a small part of the infinite Dharma the Buddha has given in the Lotus Sutra.

It isn't possible to welcome all the gods and Buddhas from the infinite past to the infinite future from all directions of the infinite universe if we have only cleared away one chair. Where will everyone sit in such a cramped way, some may choose not to respond to your invitation at all. They may grumble saying why go, there won't be space anyway.

The space here is not however a physical space it is a space of mind. If we enter our place of practice as if it were the door to the entire universe and our dusting and changing water and offerings is the equivalent of preparing a grand banquet with copious snacks and drinks, then this is the place the Buddhas and gods from the ten directions will eagerly wish to visit. With one's whole being one engages in these actions from the mind of the great expanse of space and time then one's life throughout the day expands far beyond the bounds of trifles and trivia.

17

From the outside it may all look the same, yet from the inside the eye can not see from one end of the horizon to the other. From the outside it may appear there are mere inches between your nose and the great mandala but from the inside your body and voice reverberate throughout the entire infinite universe. That distance is not measurable yet it is all present in those few inches, if that is your mind. The difference exists solely within one's self.

And so, every yarn thread of your carpet, every splinter of wood in the floor are all dharma threads and splinters. That shabby thread bare carpet then is transformed to a grand hand woven carpet on which the Buddhas walk barefooted and in luxury. Whether the pillars be concrete or wood matters not as they are all transformed into the Dharma-realm by your life.

The pillars and posts and support structure of the place of practice is comparable to your Dharma-nature, and the strength of your faith and practice. Without a strong practice, including study, then there is only a weak structure to support your faith. Entering or approaching your practice space is an opportunity to strengthen your faith, your practice is not only supported by the beams and pillars of the space, it is also supported by the "beams" and "pillars" of your practice.

The walls represent the Dharma-realm and as I previously stated they are not merely the physical confines of the actual place you are practicing in, they represent the expansive infinite universe of Buddhism. It is only your mind that places limits on the space. As you gaze upon your practice space imagine that entire universe existing within.

The nails and planks are as if the sands of the river Ganges is laid out before you, where as the roofing material covers and protects the vastness of space. This space is so large that it will comfortably allow innumerable Buddhas and bodhisattvas and other heavenly beings to be present, as many as the sands of the Ganges.[2] Your vision can be that of a mere mortal looking through human eyes or that of a practitioner of the great Dharma of the Lotus Flower Sutra. In one case you see only as far as your eyesight in the other case you can see as far as the Buddha when he emits a ray of light from between his eyebrows.

Let your seeing be like the light of a candle which shines through darkness and illuminates the treasure land. Let your mind be as if the fragrance of incense spreading to the past, present, and future.

Now tell me honest, wouldn't you rather practice in such a grand space or if you are content to remain locked into a practice space you take for granted and ignore and treat as secondary to all else? Most would probably say the former over the later, yet how do our actions compare? The subject and the object are inseparable. If the place where you practice is not the Buddha land then the Buddha is not present practicing.

The Shutei Hoyo Shiki says:

> "You should know this place of practice is the inconceivable sphere [of activity] of all Buddhas."[3]

---

2 Shutei Hoyo Shiki - Udana-in Nichiki - page 390
3 Shutei Hoyo Shiki - Udana-in Nichiki - page 390

Contemplation on Bowing to the Three Treasures

Rai Sanbo Kan

Not sure about your mind, but if it is anything like mine, it is at times full of all kinds of stuff. There's good stuff and bad stuff and stuff I don't know quite what to do with, though I'm hoping I figure it out soon. When I've taught folks in detox to meditate almost to a person the common plea is: "I can't get my mind to stop thinking. How can I make it stop?" For all those thoughts, there is one truth underlying it all: Our minds contain the Three Jewels of Buddha, Dharma, and Sangha. In any single thought moment your mind encompasses all Dharma qualities and pervades all realms.

That's a powerful statement worthy of deep reflection. What kind of Dharma qualities are in our thoughts? Yes, that's the rub. What kind of Dharma qualities are we manifesting in our thinking? The good, the bad, and the ugly all reflect our Dharma quality. The ten worlds are always present, and the ten worlds always have each of the ten worlds present in some form. So even your bad stuff is Dharma, and so is your good stuff. The key to our practice is not to suppress or hide from those less-than-admirable thoughts but to see where they come from, examine them, and then manifest our actions from the mind of the Buddha, from the heart of the Buddha.

The principal of the Three Jewels being present in our one mind is the basis of the sutras. It is not incidental, nor did it arise after the sutras. It is the fundamental truth on which the sutras arose. The Sangha, both in body and in mind, has protected the Buddha Dharma throughout all time and spreads it all over the world and the infinite universe.

In our own Saha world, it is we – the common mortals, full of defilements, discursive thoughts, fleeting attention spans – who are tasked with spreading the Dharma. Gods or deities aren't spreading it. It is you and I, with all our imperfections, who are the most qualified to teach the Dharma to others, showing with our lives that there is a way to end suffering and attain enlightenment, as promised in the Lotus Sutra.

It is our minds that the Buddhas respond to. Our minds reveal our true self. It is easy to speak great words. It is exceedingly more difficult to keep the good words in one's mind and heart. One need only consider one's own mind and heart to see the answer to why certain things keep occurring, things we don't necessarily wish to keep happening. It isn't an easy exercise, and it isn't always pleasant to reflect on one's mind and heart. It can show some nasty stuff or at least some undesired stuff that we might rather not see. Yet it is by repeatedly examining this that change begins. Buddhism demands honesty to ourselves. You don't need to bring it out to the attention of anyone except yourself. That's hard enough.

For all that gunk that hangs around in our hearts and minds there is something else there. This something else is not to be taken lightly and should never be forgotten. Our minds, while being perceived by the Buddhas, also contain the perception of the Buddhas. Our minds are also the minds of

Buddhas. No matter how bad you may think you are, you are indeed a Buddha and possess the mind of the Buddha within your mind. The trick, as always, is to tap into it while working on lessening those other qualities that work against the Buddha in our lives.

_____

> "The innumerable great virtues of the Dharma-realm is where the Three Treasures and all human and heavenly beings abide and what the Dragon King looks up to in reverence. These Three Treasures are not only of great benefit and win over all sentient beings but are also of the same nature and entity as us.[1]"

I have in the past and continue to this day to stress the importance of the Sangha. Without the Sangha the Three Treasures do not exist. Sangha is a dynamic community, and not simply an association with or belonging to a social platform of exchanged monologues. Social media is not inherently bad, but it is not automatically a substitute for Sangha.

First, in a Sangha there is a dynamic process at work. This process is dynamic because it happens at once and not one at a time. When you enter an activity with a Sangha your presence alters the environment and causes reactions and interactions of others present in the Sangha. The activity is forever impacted by your presence and even your absence. That is why for my online digital Sangha I task everyone with participating by speaking, asking questions, responding to other's comments, as well as showing one's face by video stream. What you hear and what you say all change the

1. Shute Hoyo Shiki - Udana-in Nichiki -Page 391

experience for not only yourself but for others. Sangha is about a shared experience and a sharing experience.

Second, a Sangha is somewhat like a family sitting together at meal time. It is an opportunity to come together, even with people you haven't chosen to come together with and may not associate with at any other time. A Sangha is not merely a gathering of like-minded people. In the Sangha, people share a common objective to practice the Dharma together, help one another, encourage one another, and even disagree with one another.

I recall the evening meals my family shared nearly every day I lived at home. We didn't get along all the time, although difficult matters were mostly set aside during meals. Most of the time, however, meals were happy and sometimes even boisterous. There was always plenty of milk in the jug that my dad kept on the floor beside his chair. I liken that jug of milk to the wonderful benefit of the Lotus Sutra, always there, limitless, and easy to acquire. That milk always tasted good. Even though I continue to drink milk at all my home meals, it isn't quite the same as the milk poured from that jug.

The milk I drink in solitude is good. It is to me what makes a meal a meal. The milk in solitude though does not have the same memory nor the same experience as the milk beside my dad's chair. Sometimes the meal was consumed in an ill-tempered silence, but even in those times there was always unlimited milk. More than anything else, that milk, in my mind, was the golden elixir or ambrosia, the nectar of the gods.

Third, a Sangha provides an environment of immediate nourishment and encouragement. Of course, we may not always want to share our concerns. The sharing of one's problems is built on a trust in those with whom you share. In a physical Sangha that trust is built over time and by experimenting with problems of a less personal nature. Given enough time the sharing can become deeper and the trust continue to build. The dynamic nature of Sangha expands because of trust, contribution, respect, and a realization that we all are very much alike and much less different than we sometimes think.

I will admit that I do not participate widely in social media and so am no expert. But judging from the studies on social media I am aware of and my own experiences, I am not convinced that social media can provide the same experience one gets from a dynamic Sangha. One of my chief criticisms is the environment of monologue. While I have seen some deep and caring postings and responses, it still happens one event at a time and lacks a dynamic presence of concerned individuals coming together for the sole specific purpose of practicing the Dharma and participating in Sangha with the Buddha.

The Three Treasures of Buddha, Dharma, and Sangha are not only beneficial for each of us. They also benefit all sentient beings. The benefit is greater than simply to the participants in Sangha. The benefit expands outward to our whole environment, affecting all with whom we interact. In this time of increased silos of shared likes and a decrease in interactions with those not like us, the Sangha can serve as a model of how to get along and to work together to solve shared problems.

Many of the Shomyo, or Buddhist hymns that priests sing, contain the phrase "I shin kyo rai" (Jpn), which means "with our whole heart we bow." With our whole heart we bow to the Three Treasures, not the One Treasure, not the Two Treasures, but to all Three Treasures.

> *"Our own bowing and the Buddhas who are bowed to are all originally within one mind in which there is no bowing and no one to receive it. Although there is no bowing and no one to receive it there is certainly the response of the Buddhas and the receptivity of the ordinary people.[2] "*

The ten directions – north, east, south, west; the four intermediate directions; and the zenith and nadir – encompass all the conditions of the mind. There is no separation between our mind and the entirety of the universe.

There is no division or distinction between ourselves and others around us. The differentiation arises from the manifestation of our unique karmas. There is really no way to separate ourselves from others when it comes to Buddhist principles as we are all part of a collective environment that would be dramatically altered if even one person were absent. Our seemingly unique existence is not simply dependent upon our presence, but rather exists because of the presence of others with ourselves. We cannot become happy alone. If all around us are suffering, then we too suffer. It is possible to manifest the Buddha's land in our environment because we can also affect the potential for the Buddha land to be manifest in the lives of others.

Our mind encompasses the entire universe even if we choose

2. Shute Hoyo Shiki - Udana-in Nichiki -page 391

to ignore it. Simply being unaware or disinclined to be aware does not remove us from the reality. The same is also true of every other person. This does not mean that we know all the inner workings of the universe or have the answers to every problem. It does mean that we have the capacity to tap into the vast cosmos, the wisdom of the Buddhas of the past, present, and future. We have all that potential within us.

Practicing the Lotus Sutra allows us to first see and experience and then open to the vast treasures of the universe. The Buddha, a common mortal, a prince from a small tribe in ancient India, did just that very thing. As a result, here we are today, some 2,500 years or so removed from him, and yet we can benefit from the insight and enlightenment he gained. The path is revealed to us in this very teaching. Rather than keep it to himself, rather than dilute it, rather than change it, he gave it to us in the form of the Lotus Sutra.

When you engage in your daily practice, however it manifests, do you approach your devotion with the awareness of the greatness of the teaching and your incredible fortune to have been exposed to this profound teaching? Nothing that has come along in my life has come close to the greatness of the Lotus Sutra. It is unimaginable that I should have been exposed to it in this lifetime. A seemingly chance encounter in a military barracks only a few nights before Christmas has led me on a path that has given me fortune beyond what I could have imagined at the time. Even now, having lived it, I still find it hard to believe.

For me, bowing when there is no bowing means that all my life is both an expression of gratitude and an attempt to repay the favors I have received. Bowing when there is no one to bow to means that, when I succeed in living according to the principle that all beings possess Buddha nature, then even if people do not seem to respond their lives are forever impacted and the Buddha within them bows. Their receptivity is not dependent upon their knowledge or awareness; the Buddha within is always receptive. The one mind of self always abiding in the Lotus Sutra is far reaching and encompassing. The one mind abiding in the Lotus Sutra speaks to the one mind of every being in the universe and so the universe abides in us and bows to us.

On Reciting the Sutra

Ju Kyo Mon

"When we chant the sutra all the heavenly dragons, the eight kinds of supernatural beings, the monks, nuns, laymen, and laywomen will all gather round to listen. When we become a Dharma-master we must understand that we are to convey the True Dharma and teach the four kinds of devotees. After we finish chanting the sutra we must pray that in the future we will attain awakening together with all sentien beings by this merit.[1]"

It cannot be said often enough that chanting the sutra yields immeasurable benefits. I think we all know that or at least we all say we know that. How deeply aware of that are we in the depths of our lives? Perhaps some say this is true and yet find a space in their lives that is unsure. I don't think there is anything broken in you if you harbor those doubts. Nope, nothing wrong with you at all. In fact, it is perhaps more normal than not.

Too often in matters of faith it is supposed that true faith is a faith without the slightest doubt or questioning. Because of this people often fear revealing the truth of their lives.

1   Grand Master T'ien-t'ai Chih'i from Kanjin-jukyo-ho (The Way of Contemplative Recitation) Shutei Hoyo Shiki page 392

29

As a result everyone wanders around thinking they must be the only one who doubts. It is as if we don't want to reveal the chink in our armor, fearing that the next person will use that to accuse us of not having a "pure, undoubting faith," whatever that might look like.

I like to think of those moments of doubt and questions as exciting places. They are places of discovery and invite curiosity. When we can relish our doubts, we can humanize our beliefs and our practice. Pure faith – again whatever the heck that is – is inhuman. It isn't approachable. I mean seriously, how do you relate to someone who is perfect? I would expect the person wearing a sandwich board advertising their perfection to be trying to sell me snake oil and not something that really works. The person with doubts and yet being quite human, on the other hand, would be someone I could relate to.

My doubts center around whether I am qualified to teach others about the Dharma. Who am I to think I have any claim to wisdom or knowledge beyond what everyone else has long ago sorted out? I also have doubts about whether I am offering anything of value with regard to understanding and practicing the Lotus Sutra. I'm not fishing for compliments or assurances. I'm instead letting you peek inside my mind.

Since I've been writing I've had numerous people say complimentary things about how what they read helped them understand and have a deeper relation to their practice of the Lotus Sutra. I am left speechless, often fearing that if I say anything it will ruin the illusion. Yet I am also aware that what they say is true, and they are being sincere. I am thankful that I can have such an ability, though I am doubtful that I can claim it as my own. I know that it only comes from my faith in and practice of the Lotus Sutra. Even if unskilled, it is still my wish to somehow share with and encourage others to find the joy I have found, not exactly like mine but their own version.

When we recite the sutra, we should do so with a clear voice, strong and confident, clear and melodic. In my writing this is how I hope to be. Whether you write, draw, make music, add up numbers on a spreadsheet, direct planes in an airport, guard resources, answer telephones, field consumer complaints on a hotline, report the news, care for children, make babies, arrange flowers, collect the refuse of humanity, test water quality, drive a bus, guard the cross walk for children, represent voters as a politician, litigate matters before a judge, carry a weapon in combat, train for combat, and on and on the list could go – you have an opportunity to sing the phrases of the Lotus Sutra with the very actions of your task. This is how we can recite the sutra with our lives.

Reciting the sutra traditionally means doing so from memory whereas reading is the actual eyes on paper reading, either aloud or silently. When we do our daily service, we are encouraged not to recite but to read, as this ensures we don't take shortcuts or mispronounce the words. Of course, we can recite, but we should be mindful of checking our recitation frequently to ensure we remain faithful to the words of the text.

Our actions are an opportunity to recite the sutra with our lives. We have a choice as to whether our actions are melodic, in harmony with the situation and task at hand, or whether they will be discordant and at odds with our environment. Harmony yields joy; disharmony yields discomfort. When we are in harmony with the Lotus Sutra, it makes it easy for others to enter the wonderful benefits of the Dharma even without being aware of those benefits. This the Buddha responds to, this their Buddha nature responds to and this awakens the seed to their enlightenment. There is nothing we need to do but provide the nutrients to the awakening of their Buddha nature.

The notion of converting people, or convincing them to take faith in the Lotus Sutra, is at odds with the belief that everyone possesses a Buddha nature within their lives. Seriously, what is there I can convince someone of, or convert them to, if they are already a Buddha? Rather it is incumbent on me to provide the fertile field for their Buddha nature to sprout and grow from within their lives. Conversion is a mind game and one of dominance. It is operating from a mindset of superiority and subjugation, which is contrary to everything in the Lotus Sutra.

The other day one of the members of the Sangha asked a question about chanting the Sutra in English. He said it didn't seem melodic or have the same effect as chanting the Shindoku, the traditional Japanese pronunciation of the Chinese characters. Another member of the Sangha shared that when he recites in English he modulates his voice as he would normally when reading. He adds emphasis to the parts he feels moved to emphasize, raises the pitch of his voice when so moved, much like when he read to his son as a child.

I fully support this way of reciting in English for your personal practice. The monotone voice is a Japanese traditional sensibility, and when we read in group adopting a monotone voice is appropriate. Still, adopting a more natural manner in our English recitation is supported within the Hoyo Shiki, which I'll talk more about in a later section on vocal quality. Briefly though, we as priests are encouraged to be melodic and not unnatural or unpleasing.

> *"With a scattered mind you cannot chant the Lotus Sutra, nor can you enter into the concentration meditative absorption. Concentrate and be mindful of each word of the Lotus Sutra when you practice it whether sitting or standing. If you accomplish this practice you will see the body of Universal Sage Bodhisattva.[2]"*

What I'm about to say won't end the debate over whether chanting or sutra reciting is meditation, yet I am going to once again say that in every way it is as much meditation as anything is, including silent sitting. Silent sitting and all the permutations of mindfulness practice are mostly a Western phenomena. Silent meditation is not now nor has it ever been a primary practice for Buddhists. Even today the most common form of practice is sutra chanting. This is not a Japanese thing. This is a Buddhist thing.

Those who lightly toss off notions of chanting as being meditative haven't fully engaged in a practice that has challenged them to go beyond their comfort zone. For many it is the pitfall of Buddhism of Convenience. When it becomes inconvenient they lose their attention. Chanting the sutra is extremely difficult, and even more so if one tries to maintain a concentrated mind. Try chanting Odaimoku for 10 minutes and see how prone your mind is to wander. It isn't because chanting hinders meditation. It's because

---

2 Grand Mater Nan-yüeh Hui-ssu, Hokekyo-anrakugoy-gi (Annotations on the Peaceful Practices Chapter of the Lotus Sutra) Shutei Hoyo Shiki, page 392

chanting challenges you to concentrate your mind in ways that silence and sitting in groups of individuals isolated in their own minds does not. Chanting and reciting are difficult enough as a solitary practice and the challenge is 10-fold harder in a group.

The concentration one can achieve by chanting can elevate the mind and life condition in ways I do not believe silent sitting can. The transcendent effect of meditation is multiplied when the mind is carried into the heart of the sutra or Odaimoku through concentrated meditative active presence.

In group chanting or reciting it is not only your voice, it is your voice along with other voices. You are a part of and not isolated from the experience. You both give and receive. You contribute, and you partake. Your voice naturally seeks harmony with the group voice. Your ears hear the voices of others as well as your modified voice. Your voice you hear is not the same voice the others hear and what you hear of others is not what they hear of themselves. Your listening does not diminish nor lessen the sounds others are making. It is like a candlelight that is not diminished because it lights other candles. And the light of a candle can illuminate darkness without being consumed, regardless of how long the darkness has persisted.

To chant the sutra together with others requires courage. We don't often think of that. Think back to your first time chanting in group. If you were like most people you were shy, hesitant, and even afraid. You probably were hyper-aware of your voice, and most likely you were the only one so aware of your voice. Over time those fears became less and you perhaps now gladly and with confidence join your voice with others in recitation. Just because you are more confident now does not mean you don't have courage when you chant. Your lack of awareness of the courage it takes to chant is merely a function of your practice and continually shoring up your courage.

I'm guessing the first time you recited the sutra alone you were just as shy and timid as in a group. To chant the sutra takes incredible courage. The sutra talks about the roar of the lion, yet when we first start chanting a lion is not what would come to mind for many. Over time you overcame those doubts and fears, you were manifesting the behavior of a lion, though you probably didn't think about it at the time. The lion is fearless, and over time you become fearless in your recitation.

The lion, besides being fearless, focuses on the task at hand. So too, even though we may be confident in our recitation and chanting Odaimoku, we need to remain focused on the sutra, the task at hand, acquiring the nourishment of the Dharma.

> "If a Phrase of the sutra fills your heart it will be an aid to reaching the other shore. By deeply reflecting on and mastering the Dharma it will become a great vessel for crossing over. Being able to see and hear the Dharma follows upon it's joyful reception, as a vassal always follow after his lord. Whether somebody accepts this teaching or abandons it, they will form a causal connection with it through hearing. Whether somebody follows it or goes against it, they will finally be able to achieve liberation through hearing it."

It is noteworthy that the quote above does not say,

"When you have memorized a phrase," nor does it
say, *"When you have comprehended a phrase.*[3]*"*

Instead it says when your heart is full of the sutra, that is
when you have joy and excitement, even irrationally. With
that joy you have the tool you need to liberate yourself from
suffering.

To reflect on the Dharma certainly engages the mind, but
it isn't generally thought of as heart-centered. Know what
makes your heart sing. All too often in life we ignore the
heart, and even more frequently we fail to hear the quiet
whispers there. The mind shouts with a loud voice. Only in
introspection can we create space for the voice of the heart
and our connection to the spirit of the universe.

When we have great joy, the sutra says in Chapter II, we will
become Buddhas. Joy is not a mental phenomenon. Miao-lo
says that being able to see and hear the Dharma is connected
to our joyful reception. These ancient wise Dharma masters
had an admirable passion for the Dharma. Their passion
seems so great that you would be greatly influenced simply
by being in their presence, even if you didn't understand a
word they spoke.

There is something about being passionate that radiates in a
person. It is certainly different from someone who is well-
versed but passionless. I think back to the story I was told
when I first began practicing Nichiren Buddhism. It was
about two brothers who were so intellectually challenged
they didn't even know their own names, and would answer to

---

3 Venerable Ching-hsi (aka Miao-lê Chan-jan), Hokke-
mongu-ki (Annotations on the Words and Phrases of the
Lotus Sutra) Shutei Hoyo Shiki, page 392

the name of their brother before answering to their own. Or the story of someone who recently converted to Buddhism after meeting the Buddha. In the case of the brothers they were able to 'teach' Buddhism through their very being. In the case of the newly converted man, while traveling he met someone and converted them to Buddhism simply by saying he didn't know anything but he had met the Buddha. In both cases it was the passion that filled their lives that communicated in ways words could not.

I wonder if in our time we have somehow relegated passion to the bin or feel it inappropriate, or even substandard to intellectual mastery. It's as if intellectualism has been divorced from passion. Your words – whether eloquent or not – when coupled with your passion of faith can move people and cause them to become happy. Your passion for the Dharma and the joy it brings you can awaken the Buddha in those you meet. That little spark of your passion is like a small jolt of electricity that startles the slumbering Buddha, causing it to open its eyes and begin to seek out its full awakening. You may not see it, you may think your efforts are inconsequential, but that is the mistake of the intellect. In Chapter XXII we are told our mission is to cause people to have great joy simply by sharing any truth of the Buddha's teachings. Causing people to have great joy is not about convincing someone of some intellectual or philosophical profundity. It is about having great joy in yourself for them and the Buddha already in their lives.

None of us fully knows the route we took to have faith in Buddhism, much less the Lotus Sutra. We may know the path in this lifetime but before that, what do we know? We may have been the Walmart cashier in some distant realm of the universe who one day had someone in their check-out line who simply smiled and said thank you, wishing for you great joy. Long ago in the past our flame was ignited, and we began our search for a way to fully manifest our Buddha self. Eventually after traveling thousands of galaxies and being reborn in untold realms – sometimes as a humanoid and other times as some other being – finally we were reborn in this place, in this time, and seemingly quite by accident we came across the Lotus Sutra and took faith. Then "bam" we are here, and now what shall we do? Shall we think about it? Or shall we embrace it, feel it, be energized by it?

Hear me roar like the lion!

> *"The Buddha is the unexcelled King of the Dharma. Once we chant what he preached with his golden lips, the spiritual phrases of the sacred teachings, those words will become a Dharma-wheel that travels throughout the earth. The yakshas chant to the sky as an offering to the Four Heavenly Kings. After the Heavenly Kings hear it, they then pass it on until it reaches the King of the Brahma Heaven. This chanting spreads out to the dead and to the living. The dragon-gods are as pleased as when people listen to the speech of a king. Who would not praise it? The merit of chanting is like this.[4]"*

Even though our ears are not fine-tuned and so are unable to hear many frequencies, our voices are heard and cause the universe to move. We can have a voice of love or of hate, and then what we hear in return, what we experience is in accord with our voice. Think how the universe is moved

4 Wu-chin, Goho-ron (Treatise on Protecting the Dharma) Shute Hoyo Shiki, page 393

when we recite the words of the Buddha. Even our small voice reaches the heavens.

I remember one night as a child when my parents got into an argument and started yelling at each other while I was taking a bath. My father stormed into the bathroom, grabbed some things, and turned out the lights, slamming the door on his way out. There I was alone in the bathtub in the dark. I hit my head on the water spout and got a cut which started bleeding. Maybe that's why to this day I don't like taking baths. Regardless, their voices and their actions reverberated, and were felt by me. We know the energy of angry words are powerful. I think we often discount the equal power that words of kindness have and the even greater power of our voice lifting the words and phrases in the sutra, especially the Lotus Sutra.

I wish for you great joy. This is a powerful statement. What's even more beautiful about this wish based upon the Lotus Sutra is that it doesn't contain any mention of what that joy might be. It is up to everyone to determine what their great joy is. That is why when I pray for someone who has requested a specific prayer from me I simply pray that they have the necessary resources to solve their situation. I am not capable of knowing exactly what someone needs. I can't know the specifics, but I can easily put my life energy into a prayer for the necessary resources, whatever they may be.

Contained within the teachings of the Lotus Sutra are limitless resources for us to navigate our life situation. We will never know them if we ignore reading, reciting, and studying. As Nichiren says in the Shoho Jisso Sho, "Endeavor, endeavor to strengthen your faith."

As Wu-chin says, our small voices are relayed to the King of the Brahma Heaven. And this pleases not only the living and the dead, it also pleases the Brahma King. It's always nice to make the Brahma King happy.

I feel as if I am being a bit redundant here so rather than continuing to repeat myself and the wise ancient elders I'll wrap it up by simply encouraging you to pursue with joy, with vigor, with determination the practice of reciting the sutra. Get a hold of a copy of the romanized version of the Shindoku text of the Lotus Sutra and practice reciting in this way. If you are unable to do that right now have it as an eventual goal and recite from the English a portion of the Lotus Sutra every day. Your life will change, and your faith with strengthen.

Contemplation on Reading and Reciting the Sutra

Dokuju Kyoden Kan

The Lotus Sutra begins with the phrase "Thus have I heard." We may interpret that to mean the text that follows is the teaching and in so doing ignore or pass over the title of Myoho Renge Kyo. To do so would be in error as what was heard was the title – Myoho Renge Kyo – with the text following in explanation. The title is the teaching.

Both the title and the text are deeply connected and both are necessary. Myoho Renge Kyo is the key to open a locked door; the following 28 chapters are what is to be opened. To consider one separately from the other would be like trying to enter your home through a locked door without pulling the key out of your pocket and inserting it into the lock. While it is true that you have the key, without actually utilizing it you will have difficulty entering your home. Even in the case of my electronic lock, without either the key or my cell phone the magic of automatic entry or backup manual entry is not possible. Like my electronic door lock, which automatically unlocks when I pull into my driveway, the benefits of the Lotus Sutra come to us when we both practice and study, even without our full understanding. This is faith.

Every phrase, every character of the Lotus Sutra is contained in Myoho Renge Kyo. The five Chinese characters contain every stroke and every mark of all the 69,384 characters comprising the Lotus Sutra. All of the virtues of the entire 28 chapters of the text are all contained within the five characters of the title. Every single character within the text of the sutra contains all the virtues of the five character title. Neither is too small, nor too large. Neither is required to expand or contract to accommodate or fill the other. Every character produces virtue due to its relationship with and inclusion of all the other characters. To ignore the text or to ignore the title deprives us of the mutual benefit of the two together. I imagine this much like the relationship of beans and rice. Both contain protein yet when combined the total protein is greater than the sum of their individual proteins. That is perhaps why, even without understanding the science of protein analysis, you can find some version of a beans and rice combination food staple in cultures throughout the world. And so it is with the characters of the title of the sutra and the body text.

"Each character produces virtue just as the wish-fulfilling jewel constantly rains down many other jewels. Even one jewel is enough, while 10,000 jewels are not too many. No matter the quantity what is produced in sufficient. You should know that each character and sound spreads throughout the Dharma-realm to propagate the Buddha's teaching in the past, present, and future, bringing benefit to all beings.[1]"

As we practice reading and reciting the sutra the place we are in – the place in which we practice our devotion to the Lotus Sutra – is where the Three Treasures of the ultimate truth of the Buddha appear. It is also the place where the protective forces of the universe accept our offering of the

---

1. Shutei Hoyo Shiki page 394

Verses for Joyfully Upholding the Sutra

Chokyo Ge

The word ge means verse, or similar to a free form poem. In Chinese the lines are generally of 5 characters or, as we might hear it, five syllables. For an example of this you can look at the section of Chapter XVI we recite in our daily service. We refer to this section as the Ji Ga Ge, an abbreviated name which is derived from the first two characters with ge or verse added. The Shute Hoyo Shiki does not present this section as a verse, and I wonder if perhaps something is lost to us in the translation into English.

What is presented sounds like it could have been or was a verse. It's not very long so I'll include it in its entirety.

"Chapter one of the Annotations on the Words and Phrases of the Lotus Sutra says, 'The calling of the Wonderful Dharma is not just the main part of the sutra. All the 28 chapters together are called wonderful. That is why each chapter contains the entity and each phrase converges in the wonderful name.' We bow to Myoho Renge Kyo, the Saddharma-pundarika, in one set with 8 fascicles, 28 chapters, and 69,384 characters. Each character is a true Buddha. The preaching of a true Buddha benefits all sentient beings. Therefore, all sentient beings have already attained the Buddha Way. That is why we

bow to the Lotus Sutra.[1]"

When we carry out our practice of the Lotus Sutra, when we venerate the Lotus Sutra, when we bow to or lift the sutra, we are doing all of these things not simply because of the word Wonderful in the title. Everything contained within the sutra is wonderful. It is a collection of wonderfulness. Each of the 69,384 Chinese characters that comprise the text of the sutra is a Buddha and each of those Buddhas benefits us. We bow to each of them when we bow to the Lotus Sutra.

Our practice, as I've mentioned previously, is larger, much larger, and more significant than we appreciate as we recite the sutra. We are no small speck of life in an infinite universe. We are grand and noble beings whose thoughts, voice, and actions reverberate across the cosmos, witnessed by all the Buddhas of the past, present, and future. These actions are witnessed and heard by every deity, every protective force, and even Mara King Devil. Our voice vibrates endlessly far beyond the space in which we are chanting, far beyond the walls surrounding us, far beyond the building, and even further still beyond our solar system.

When we can begin to shift our self-awareness to the grandeur of our actions as connected with and expressed toward the Lotus Sutra, then our lives begin to shift and expand. It is as if you sometimes feel like your physical body is not large enough. At times I've almost felt like I might explode.

Recent scientific studies exploring the effect of the mind's thoughts on the actions being performed at the time have shown that when the mind thinks an activity is exercise and not simply work or chores, then the body burns more calories

---

1. Sutei Hoyo Shiki page 395

and muscles actually gain strength more so than if we hold in our mind thoughts of chores or tedium. Walking to the bathroom, an action we may do mindlessly, when thought of as walking exercise burns more calories than mindlessly walking to relieve one's bladder. These are small things, yet show how powerful the mind is and how important framing our thoughts can be.

What we hold in our mind, or what our mind thinks about the things the body does, has great importance. It is quite something to think that thousands of years ago the saints and sages in Buddhism knew this. It is also quite something how many miss the importance of what the mind thinks about your reciting the sutra and chanting the Odaimoku.

When I lead chanting at my temple I always tell people as we begin to "chant with great joy and confidence." Why do I do this? It is because I've experienced the difference. I can feel the difference from chanting with joy and confidence deep down in my life. Even if my voice is weak, as it sometimes is now as I age, in my mind, in my heart, I hold the thought of strength, confidence, and joy.

When we can approach our practice with the thought that what we are doing is huge, it is phenomenal, it is significant, it is powerful, and we are doing this thing and we are a part of it and we are making it happen in our lives, that is when we can begin to approach the tremendous joy that the Lotus Sutra holds for us. The Lotus Sutra is there waiting for us to enter and enter in a big way.

If you opened your front door tomorrow morning and standing outside were 69,384 Buddhas, would you simply shrug your shoulders and rush on by saying merely 'hey guys, gotta run?' Seriously, would you? You may think this is ludicrous, and if so that's where your mind is. All those Buddhas are there every morning, every afternoon, every evening, and every night.

Are your devotions carried out in a small 8-foot by 10-foot room, or in a grand hall so large you cannot see the four walls, so bright from all the gold, silver, and gems you almost need sunglasses?

These may seem silly, yet the difference in your thoughts about what you are doing is important and significant.

Shodai Kan

For those who may be new to Nichiren Buddhism, or any Buddhism for that matter, when you enter the practice hall you may see various statues, or simply a scroll with paintings or calligraphy. I've been asked by non-Buddhists about the statues, and almost always the question leads to the notion of worshiping idols.

Many people from all walks of life and from various cultures practice Buddhism. There is no one single practice or even belief. Some people may and do pray to the statues as a representation of a benevolent force to intercede on their behalf to resolve some important matter in their life. Is that wrong? In some ways it's the wrong question.

A better question might be whether the practice of praying to some representation of an entity in hopes of receiving some assistance is harmful or helpful. The answer may be different for the same person at different times and under different circumstances.

In times of extreme crisis, people often reach out to, even grasp at, anything that will bring them hope. That same person in a different situation may realize that the image is merely a reminder or stimuli to focus one's efforts of faith and practice. The wrist mala I wear is not magical, though it could be in the right situation. It is, however, a constant reminder that I say I believe in Buddhism and that my actions should be reflected upon to verify that they are indeed in accord with what I say from my mouth. This is the function of my wrist mala for me. But calling it just a reminder would be an understatement of its significance, since I would not think to discard it casually, nor treat it disrespectfully. It means more to me than just a reminder. It's complicated.

When we place faith in our practice, what best represents our faith is our actions. If, in our prayers, we somehow believe we are no longer responsible for taking appropriate actions on our own behalf, or that we no longer need to change our patterns of behavior, then our prayers are misguided and potentially harmful.

I frequently recall a book I read many years ago at the suggestion of a Rabbi friend entitled The Seventh Telling by Mitchell Chefitz. In this book the teller of the tale, a Jewish mystic, talks about inappropriate prayers. Suppose on your way home you see a house on fire in the distance. The house is in the general direction of your very own residence. At this distance you are unable to discern if the fire is your house or another. An inappropriate prayer – and an impossible prayer – would be to pray that the fire isn't in your house. The fire is already burning. It is either your house or it isn't. Your prayer will not change the location of the fire.

He also writes of a beautiful example of how prayer is sometimes a negotiation. You want red widgets, but the factory only has yellow and green widgets. You can't have red widgets. Praying for red widgets is pointless. They don't have any, and they're not going to make any. You can have yellow or green, or leave empty handed. Life is like that.

From my time as a hospital chaplain I recall a mother who, no matter how hard she prayed, could not change the medical certainty that her 18-year-old son would soon die. I shall never forget the week I spent with the mother and father. Medically, death was certain. Over the course of the week, as the mother prayed and read her Bible, she realized that, for her, the answer to her prayers lay in becoming at peace with the reality, being able to let her son breathe his last breath, and accept that nothing will ever be the same. I could not bring her to such a place. She had to find and walk that path herself. I could witness and accompany her so she was not alone, and honor her journey toward a continued life while her son took his journey into death. His death was beautiful, if any death can be. The boy's mother, father, and siblings were all present, as was I at their invitation. Together we all stood around his bed. When I told the doctors the family was ready, they disconnected the "machines." Within minutes he breathed his last breath as we all wept. It was sad. It was terribly sad. It is the way of life. Many of his organs were used to enhance the lives of people throughout the United States, though that is a small comfort. It's like second place, or settling for yellow or green widgets.

Whether a person prays to a statue or a piece of paper or prays to nothing is a personal question.

When you enter a Buddhist hall you may see many statues, or none at all. In the case of an Image Hall or Founder's Hall, the statue or picture is not of someone to worship, but is for honoring or venerating the founder of the sect or lineage.

When I lived at Joen-ji in Shinjuku, Tokyo, I attended a lecture in the basement of the Founder's Hall given by a speaker from a different Nichiren denomination. During the lecture the speaker mistakenly offered as proof that Nichiren Shu worshiped Nichiren the fact that there was a life-size statue of Nichiren in the hall above. The hall, however, was a place where few services were held. It was a place where novice priests practiced their sutra recitation and chanted abundant Odaimoku in preparation for Shingyo Dojo. On special occasions marking various persecutions in Nichiren's life all the priests would go there, sit upon special straw mats guaranteed to cut your insoles to shreds and offered prayers commemorating the persecution. I can attest that those special straw mats are not made of straw. They are in fact razor blades disguised as straw. They are deadly.

The point I'm making is that the Image Hall or Founder's Hall is not a place of regular services or daily practice. Where the practice or service takes place is in the Main Hall or Hondo. This is where you will see not one statue of some guy but lots of statues of various beings. In the case of Nichiren Buddhism, and in larger temples such as Joen-ji, there can be a statue for every being on the mandala Nichiren created to represent the Lotus Sutra's ceremony in the air.

The original function of the oldest established temples in Buddhism was to recreate the environment representing the most important teaching of that particular denomination. In the 4th, 5th and 6th centuries, rather than having statues, entire rooms would be painted to represent an important teaching. The practitioner enters into the mandala. There are some wonderful examples of rooms painted as the Diamond Sutra or the Lotus Sutra. The idea is to provide a sense of being immersed in the sutra. So it is with the statues and the calligraphic mandala used in Nichiren Shu. Our handicap in the West is that we don't automatically recognize the beings represented by the written characters. With the statues, we can see an image.

In Nichiren Buddhism, whether using calligraphy on paper or statues, we are not some disconnected observer. On the calligraphic mandala we are gazing up at the two Buddhas, Shakyamuni and Taho, seated on either side of the Odaimoku, which represents the great stupa in the ceremony in the air. On either side of the two Buddhas are the Four Great Bodhisattvas, leaders of the Buddha's original disciples, who rose up from under the ground. Everyone else depicted on the mandala is looking up at the two Buddhas. We join this gathering when we gaze upon the mandala.

In some ways there is no ceremony until we join. Everyone in the congregation – every character on the paper mandala, every wooden statue – is waiting on you to begin the ceremony. The ceremony is being held just for you. They could have finished up 3,000 years ago, but at the request of the Buddha they have waited. The Buddha told them someone of great importance was coming and now finally you have arrived. Go to them and tell them you are ready to begin the ceremony in the air.

Whether the focal point of your gazing or veneration is a mandala Gohonzon or a statue arrangement Gohonzon, there is no doctrinal distinction. They are all equal. In Nichiren Shu, there are five versions of the object of worship that are recognized: a full statue arrangement, a full calligraphic scroll, the single phrase Namu Myoho Renge Kyo, a statue of the Buddha, a statue of the Buddha and Namu Myoho Renge Kyo. Each is equal to the others. Never fear that because you don't have all the statues you are somehow missing out. Regardless of which one you have or if you have none, it is your faith and practice that is most important.

The Odaimoku in the center of the Mandala Gohonzon is manifesting the entity of the Original Buddha in our mind. As such, it contains all the Buddhas of the ten directions – the four cardinal points, the intersections between each, and the zenith and nadir. It also contains all the sentient beings of all the Dharma realms, the lands of those realms and, in fact, everything in them. In other words, everything is contained in and embraced by Namu Myoho Renge Kyo.

There is no division between us and them or self and other. Namu Myoho Renge Kyo manifests what's in our mind and everything beyond our minds from the perspective of the Original Buddha. The trick is for us to operate from that perspective of the Original Buddha within us. That's incredibly difficult to maintain in every moment of one's life. It's not impossible; just hard. There is no easy path to enlightenment, as you can see. The work of the Buddha, our work, is never fully done.

If you're anything like me, most of the time I'm operating from the mind of a rather ordinary human who frequently thinks he is disconnected from most everything that isn't within eyesight. Yes, I can intellectually touch that notion of interconnectedness, but to live, go about my business, interact with countless others, well that's an entirely different matter. I do believe I'm better than I once was. I hope even better than I was yesterday. I also know I've room to grow and improve so that tomorrow I can be better than I am today.

I'm writing this on the eve of the Thanksgiving holiday in the United States. In just a little over a month from now it will be New Year's Eve. In years past on New Year's Eve

I have led a Repentance and Reflection Ceremony called Hokke Senbo. The instruction I give prior to the service is that while it is important to repent on our past transgressions, what is equally, if not more important, is to reflect on why we did whatever it was, how we might change our response next time, and how we can grow from this.

When I think of repentance or forgiveness I am drawn to the Jewish concept of repair, specifically "repair the world." As we reflect on the causes of our transgression and how we might grow and change so that we don't act unskillfully, we might also reflect on what we might do to repair any damage we caused. This is not to say we need to pick up a guilt burden, but we should reflect on this as well when we consider future actions. In all things, we seek to do the greatest good while avoiding causing harm, or causing as little harm as possible.

Think about the Odaimoku manifesting in our minds and hold the image of that Odaimoku as a great ocean. There are numerous waves, and they are formed due to a variety of causes. Some waves are the result of the gravitational pull of the moon. Various winds also cause waves. Further causes for waves are the geographic formations beneath the surface of the ocean.

Consider your mind and what sorts of waves are being created by your thoughts. In my case, my thoughts sometimes create those huge tropical storm waves and storm surge. You may, however, never make such waves. Your waves may be the gentle ones formed by gentle thoughts. Sometimes my ocean is calm and at other times it can be extremely stormy and hazardous to any ships or surfers. Other times I might get lucky and create the perfect surfing wave, and I'm imagining it on Sunset Beach in Hawaii, which by the way is a beautiful place to surf.

Consider next those murky images that are moving around beneath the surface of your ocean. Those images, some clear and some indistinct, are all products of your thoughts. Some may be benign, and others malevolent. As you chant the Odaimoku and focus your mind on the mandala, your voice, your thoughts spread out to the entire ocean of your mind. This is your chance to calm those rough seas and rid your ocean of pollution.

There is a bay on the island of Oahu, Hawaii, called Waimea Bay. The water there is crystal clear and, due to the protective rock formations around it, remains calm except in extreme weather. It is a protected environment both by nature and by government regulations. Swimming is allowed but only snorkeling and not scuba diving. The water is not deep but deeper than standing height. The bay, protected as it is, is the home to many species of tropical fish. It is such a delight to swim there and to be able to clearly see the fish swimming alongside. You can see from the surface to the bottom. Recalling the times I've been swimming there and the beautiful colors of the fish is a fond memory. This is the kind of ocean I wish to create from my Odaimoku.

The Ten Worlds are mutually possessed in the Odaimoku, and each of these Ten Worlds mutually possess all Ten Worlds. All the virtues of each of the 100 Worlds thus derived are infused in the Odaimoku and thus we receive the merit of those virtues. Our chanting helps to restore the imbalances in our lives, smoothing out the rough patches. Perhaps we've had a bad day, and we have over exercised our world of Anger. We become out-of-harmony and our world appears as an angry place. Perhaps we have become musclebound by using Anger so much. To restore balance, we need not only to be less angry, but we need to strengthen the virtues of the other worlds.

Perhaps the problem is Hunger. I'm writing this on the sales weekend following the US Thanksgiving holiday. This is a time of heavy promotion to buy stuff. All sorts of emails have been flooding my inbox with solicitations to purchase things with supposedly special sales and discount coupons. It can be tough to keep Hunger in its proper perspective. Each of the Ten Worlds can present a problem if out of balance.

When we chant Odaimoku in front of the Gohonzon, it is these things we are advised to contemplate – balance in our living, and calm and clear seas in our mind.

Next consider your environment as you experience it. In Chapter XI, Beholding the Stūpa of Treasures, Shakyamuni must recall all his manifestations from throughout the worlds of the ten directions before he can open the Stupa of Treasures and reveal the Buddha within to the congregation. Shakyamuni purifies additional nearby worlds until he finally has enough space. In removing impurities, he reveals the beautiful adornments that are inherent in each of the lands.

In this action we are taught that our world, our land, our environment is all of the lands and places throughout the entire universe. This means that our occupancy in space is connected to and part of the furthest reaches of what we think of as the solar system and even the universe. Captains Kirk, Picard, and Janeway haven't even begun to explore as far as the space we are a part of and connected to. I'm not sure it is possible to impress upon you with my words the vastness of your environment. All the countless realms, the infinite number of Buddha lands, are all contained in this land. As humble and meager as you may think your environment is, it is only an illusion.

The Odaimoku we chant contains all the Dharmas of all the Buddhas from all the realms of the universe and manifests all the pure Buddha Worlds of Tranquil Light. They are all manifest in your life through the sound of your voice chanting the Odaimoku.

> *"...When we contemplate the Original Buddha with every thought and chant the wondrous name with every utterance the inconceivable power of the wondrous name and the wondrous entity manifest itself. All delusions will be eliminated, and all merits will be achieved. Dedicate this merit so it will spread to the entire Dharma-realm and benefit all sentient beings in the depths of their minds so that they will attain the merit of the Buddha of inherent existence.[1]"*

---

1. Shutei Hoyo Shiki, Udana-in Nichiki, page 398

Endon Sho

Our devotion and the devotional phrase are a two-part deal. One part is Myoho Renge Kyo, which we all know is the Wonderful Dharma of the Lotus Flower Sutra. Picture this as a book. The book, Myoho Renge Kyo, is sitting on the coffee table or perhaps on a bookshelf. You are on the sofa, all nice and comfy. You are Namu.

At this point you can see there is a separation between you, the subject, and the book, the object. But if you go over to the bookshelf and pick up the book and hold it and begin to read it, you and the book are connecting. Now Namu is appended to Myoho Renge Kyo. Mind you, this is only an illustration.

At this point you are more connected holding the book or holding it and reading than when you were in one place and it was in another. Suppose as you read it you become emotionally involved in some part of the sutra. Say you're reading about this huge assembly of people watching the Buddha sit in meditation, and you are curious about this scene you're reading. Now you are even more connected. You, Namu, have come closer to the Myoho Renge Kyo. You are nearing an experience of oneness of subject and object.

Now let's say you're reading the sutra and you come to the guy whose children are playing inside a dilapidated house that has burst into flame. You might be a parent yourself, and you imagine what you might feel if they were your children. At this point, you have entered the Lotus Sutra even more deeply and your Namu is even more at one with the Myoho Renge Kyo. You are closer to the unification of subject and object. You are not simply becoming the Lotus Sutra, you are beginning to feel the Lotus Sutra that is fundamentally at the core of your life.

Further along you read about some folks who pop up out of the ground and have wondrous bodies. Out of the ground they come, and they keep coming in what appears to be an impossible number. And you may realize that you too came from the earth, and you too have a desire to go to and praise the Buddha just as they did. You also realize that you have been trying to tell people about the Lotus Sutra just as they promised they would. And you begin to think you are acting as they did and fulfilling the promise they made.

You, the Namu, are now even more deeply connected to the Myoho Renge Kyo, but now it is not the book you're holding but something deeper inside you. Perhaps it makes you feel warm, or even giddy at times. Or perhaps you simply feel at home. You may feel it's just right, it fits. Now you begin to experience the connection of you and your Myoho Renge Kyo, which has been activated by your Namu.

Namu is you. It is your action. Namu is from the word Namaste. Namaste means devotion, reverence, respect. Namu and Namaste are action words. Being passive is not Namu. The more your devotion, your honoring, your behaviors, your thoughts, your every sense is directed to Myoho Renge Kyo, the more the Myoho Renge Kyo of your life is activated and the more of your environment becomes Myoho Renge Kyo. But you are the key. Myoho Renge Kyo is there, it always has been, it takes you to activate it. Buddhism is not a passive religion.

We have these images of the Buddha sitting under a tree, and we think that's all we need to do. But that's only part of the story. Yes, the Buddha attained enlightenment or awakening, but only after defeating Mara. I believe that one of the toughest battles the Buddha waged against Mara was doubt.

The Buddha doubted he could teach people. Mara tempted him by playing to those doubts, first creating them and expanding them, and then by offering alternatives. Had the Buddha not gotten up from beneath the tree and gone to teach the Four Noble Truths, whatever awakening that was achieved would have meant nothing. The awakening would have died right there, and Mara would have won. The image for us to hold on to is not of the Buddha sitting under the tree. The image of the Buddha we should hold on to is a man who got up and walked. He walked wherever he could, and he taught whomever he could. He did not rest. Sitting under the tree is a misrepresentation of the Buddha and Buddhism. Buddhism requires you to participate, and to participate with your entire life. The more of your life that participates the more Myoho Renge Kyo will manifest because of your Namu.

> *"When one fixes [the mind] on the Dharma-realm [as it is], then there is not a single sight nor smel that*

is not the Middle Way. The same goes for the realm of self, the realm of Buddha, and the realm of living beings" Grand Master Miao-lê[1]

As our Namu more fully awakens our Myoho Renge Kyo and our lives manifest the fullness and truth of the Dharma, there is no distinction or separation of self and Myoho Renge Kyo. Every bit of our lives and our experiences of life more and more take on all the truth and beauty of the Lotus Sutra.

The cool thing is that as you, the subject, and Myoho Renge Kyo, the object, become more unified, you begin to experience your world differently. You begin to smell the flavor and scent of Myoho Renge Kyo. It's everywhere, and it's very pleasing, sort of like Christmas cookies. The tastes, the sights, the sensations, everything and everywhere is Myoho Renge Kyo. What's even cooler is that it was always there, you just couldn't see it, feel it, smell it, or sense it. You aren't transported anywhere. You stay where you are, but your eyes are opened. You become awakened.

All of this is not to one extreme or another. It isn't all perfect, not by any means. Your perfection might be someone else's hell. It isn't all a bummer either. It's sort of like Goldilocks. Perhaps I shouldn't use such colorful or seemingly silly language. Yet I do think it can help to illustrate and help you form a mental image of this very important concept.

There is no distinction between you and the Dharma. Your practice doesn't make you into someone else. It doesn't change who you are. What does happen is that the good or beneficial characteristics of all the Ten Worlds are

---

1. Gand Master Miao-lê, Shutei Hoyo Shiki, page 399

strengthened so that they rise above the potential negative. In other words, you reveal the greatness that lies within you, the greatness of the Bodhisattva from beneath the ground who has been taught by the Eternal Buddha since the infinite past. You become the living manifestation of the truth of the Lotus Sutra. Now the book that was sitting on the coffee table is not merely a manuscript recorded thousands of years ago, but a living document of today.

The fact that you are not transported to some new magical perfect place with no troubles is a blessing. If that were the case, you would not be in this Saha world. You would not be able to fulfill the vows of the Bodhisattvas from beneath the ground. And no one would be able to relate to you. You, with all your foibles and imagined shortcomings, are the perfect person for the role you are to play in spreading the Dharma. This, too, is the Middle Way. You are not perfect. You are just who you need to be. Awakening the Myoho Renge Kyo within your life allows all the truth of the Dharma to manifest in your life, allowing you to reveal it to others through your very real experiences.

And in truth, the realm of self, the realm of Buddhas, and the realm of living beings are all one. There is no distinction in terms of the True Dharma of the Myoho Renge Kyo. There is no you to be cast off. There is no Buddha to be taken on. There is only the one, fully awakened through your Namu, at one with Myoho Renge Kyo.

The view of a separation, even the illustration examples I've used, are all false views. I used them because that is usually the starting point where many of us began as we were introduced to Buddhism and the Lotus Sutra. Those

65

examples starting places, and where we move to is the realization of the truth of the Middle Way.

Miao-lê says:

> *"Since ignorance and defilements are themselves identical with enlightenment, there is no origin of suffering to be eradicated. Since the two extreme views are the Middle Way and false views are the right view, there is no path to be cultivated. Since samsara is identical with Nirvana, there is no cessation to be achieved.[2]"*

Further, Miao-lê says,

> *"A single, unalloyed reality is all there is, - no entities whatever exist outside of it.[3]"*

There is the Myoho Renge Kyo and there is us, but it is a mutuality. There really is no way to write it or express it. The best we can do is what Nichiren realized with Namu Myoho Renge Kyo. Remember, Ananda begins his recollection of the Sutra with "Thus have I heard." He is saying Myoho Renge Kyo is what I heard and what follows is the explanation. When we live Namu, we are not simply manifesting the words of the 28 chapters. We are in fact unifying in body, mind, and spirit our fundamental Dharma reality and revealing the Myoho Renge Kyo. In a way Myoho Renge Kyo is who we are, and everything we live and do is like the explanation of the Namu Myoho Renge Kyo.

For those who doubt their ability to teach others the Lotus

---

2. Gand Master Miao-lê, Shutei Hoyo Shiki, page 399
3. Gand Master Miao-lê, Shutei Hoyo Shiki, page 399

Sutra, or who think they are not skillful enough to explain the Lotus Sutra to others, fear not. You are Myoho Renge Kyo. All you need do is let people experience your Namu and the Myoho Renge Kyo of your life. Your words are not nearly as important as your life. Never doubt yourself and don't underestimate the power of your actions.

"You should know that there are 3,000 worlds in one thought moment within this body and land. So when [the Buddha] attained the Way, this true principle found in all bodies and all thought moments was able to spread throughout the Dharma realm." Miao-lê[4]

4. Gand Master Miao-lê, Shutei Hoyo Shiki, page 400

Two Vital Attitudes

It is possible to be so concerned with perfection when reciting the sutra especially the Shindoku, or non-English portions. I remember when I first began I would fret over my mispronunciations and because I was intent on getting it correct I kept backing up and saying the same thing over. It would take me a long time to make any progress at all. This is not all bad, in fact desiring to say it correctly should be a constant goal regardless of the length of practice. It can however be such an obsession that one either tires of trying and gives up, or one cultivates fear of making a mistake and so causes the joy of practice to vanish.

Our practice should be a joyful expression of our fortune to have been introduced to the Lotus Sutra. At first I know it is hard to find that joy, your legs ache, your running out of time, and you can't seem to get the words correct. Try though to do your best, and let perfection go.

Perfection is less important, or not even important compared to simply showing up. Being present and doing the practice is what comes first and is always most important. If you fail to do the practice, always fearful of not being perfect then nothing happens. You don't get punished for not practicing, you don't get punished for getting it wrong. The desire to get it correct should come from a place of happiness to simply be able to do something.

In the Lotus Sutra the Buddha praises the children who draw images of the Buddha in the sand with sticks and says the merit of their offering is as great as the offerings of precious jewels. What matters most is doing something, doing it joyfully, and doing it with sincerity. From the eyes of mere common mortals the offering of a sand image of the Buddha does not appear to be as great as the offering of gold statues. From the perspective of Buddhism, the sand images could be more valuable due to sincerity and joy.

Show up for your practice. Be there and be joyful.

Solemnity here refers to sincerity. Throughout our performance or participation in our daily service we should be sincere. There most likely will be times when you are doing the service because you feel like you should. You may have a mind that says today I just want to skip, I just want to sleep in, or I just don't have time. In those instances you may indeed be forcing yourself to do the daily service. That is fine, so long as that isn't your everyday attitude. If you find that the number of times you have this sort of mind then I hope you will remember that it is a warning directed to you to re-examine your faith, practice, and study.

I have found that when one of the three are out of whack then it begins to show up in the other two. Say for instance, if my study slacks off then I sometimes begin to loose the joy of practice. It's as if I forget the reasons, or fail to remind myself of the great gift I've been given. Study is an easy thing to let slip on by and it is so crucial to maintaining one's faith. With a slackening faith one has to examine ones life keenly and recall the reasons one began to practice.

As our practice progresses and the reasons for our first accepting Buddhism fade into the distance we may soon become complacent with the current status of our lives. It is possible to think that our problems are solved or that we have always been happy. We may even think that we have arrived and no other place to go in our practice. Taking time to discern with honest and frank questions and answers, studying the sutra, and rededicating ourselves to a sincere practice are vital. The spark that keeps the fire of faith burning is our chanting the Odaimoku, even when our mind is telling us we don't need to anymore. Studying the sutra to see that our lives are not just one world of tranquility, or our hungers have not all been fulfilled, and so forth show us that we have 3000 states of mind and it isn't possible to remain in one, nor desirable.

In every instance when a weakness appears in either faith, practice, or study the key to making things right again is to examine these three legs and then strengthening them. Buddhism rest upon this tripod of faith, practice, and study. You may be aware, however I'll mention it here anyway, a tripod with it's three legs is able to provide a level surface on any terrain no matter how bumpy or rocky. It would seem that four legs would be better, and sort of obvious one leg or two not good enough. But in fact three legs is the most stable configuration for achieving stability.

Even on the days when you are forcing yourself to do your practice try to cultivate a feeling of being sincere, even in your insincerity.

Since our service is an abbreviation of what goes on in the Lotus Sutra, we are in fact recreating the sutra in our practice, it is something we should do with reverence. It would be inappropriate to take it lightly or disrespectfully. How to show respect is a fluid notion, often times tied to culture, yet some things seem to be universal.

For instance books. Here in the US and perhaps all of the West we don't think too much about where we set a book. I've seen Bibles on the back ledge under the back window in cars, Bibles that are removed every Sunday for worship and put back in the window of the car afterwards. We might think nothing of this if we are unaware that other cultures treat their sacred texts differently. In Eastern countries to do something such as what I have described to a sacred text would be considered shameful.

In Japan you would never see someone put a Bible or the Sutra directly onto the floor, here in the US I'm not sure people even think about it. Rather than place the sacred, or important book onto the floor a scarf or sheet of paper is put down first and then the book on top of that. To set the text directly on the floor is considered highly disrespectful. In fact it might even happen that someone would grab the book from you and fix the problem, though usually without directly scolding you but certainly with that look your mother gives you when you've made a serious mistake.

If you think about it though for a moment it does make sense. The floor, no matter how clean is still the place you walk on. The back window of your car gets a lot of sun, or at least is less cared for than your bookshelf in your home. This text, this sacred text is supposed to be important to you, or at least I'm guessing you claim it is or you wouldn't be reading this. So if something is important you generally tend to safeguard it and care for it. The book may seem replaceable, it is relatively easy to get another one and throw the old one away. But I'm unsure that is the best mindset we could operate from.

Once you become proficient in reciting the sutra it is easy enough to speed on through it, checking off the box on your daily list of items to accomplish. That's easy to do, and is that really how we wish to cultivate and nurture our lives. Are we simply practicing this great religion so we can say we did it, or so we can make fundamental changes in our lives. Buddhism is not a box to be checked of.

Being reverential in our practice means that we are aware we are performing a sacred ceremony that began when the Buddha revealed the Lotus Sutra for all being in this Saha world. We are in essence sitting with the Buddha on Mount Sacred Eagle listening to him speak as we gaze upon the Buddhas Shakyamuni and Many Treasures, Taho Tathagata. Don't you think they deserve to be treated with the greatest respect we are able to give?

The group I fist began practicing Nichiren Buddhism with taught that for our services we should be fully dressed, not in pajamas, and freshly shaved or make-up applied. I would echo that instruction today. It would be inappropriate to do your service and eat your meal, or sip your beverage. This is a time to give your utmost, to be fully present.

Finally in all of these things it is possible to be solemn and reverential and still be joyful. These attitudes do not need to be so onerous as to crowd out the joy of performing the practice. Always be mindful of how you are engaging in your practice and examine where you might be able to improve. That is Buddhism, always striving but not grasping so tightly as to choke off your joy.

"The Raijitsu-giki states, 'According to the Makashikan (C. Mohe-zhiguan) the 25 skillful [preparations for meditation] facilitate the realization of the true principle through concrete phenomena.[1]'"

Here we focus on actual activities or actions taken in preparation for and during our worship of the Lotus Sutra. Just as singers warm up before a performance or athletes stretch before a race, we too are advised to do certain things to prepare for our Dharma practice.

Many of us have a morning routine, a set of tasks or activities we do when we wake up to get our day going and signal to our bodies that sleep time is over, it's now time to function. Some of us also have a routine for bedtime to aide in our transition from the activities of the day to the restful and restorative slumber necessary for our survival. In fact, if we look closely enough we may see we have many rituals we carry out throughout the day as we change from one task to another.

We should not be surprised then to learn that there are suggested actions to take to benefit fully from the True Dharma of the Lotus Sutra.

---

1. Shutei Hoyo Shiki, page 204

Of the seven skillful means taught in Nichiren Shu, five are derived from the Raijitsu-giki.

From the Raijitsu-giki:

1.   Displaying the object of worship or Honzon: Nichiren Shu authorizes five ways of representing the Honzon. (I've covered this on page number 57, in Contemplation on Chanting Odaimoku chapter). The example here is when Many Treasures Buddha invites Shakyamuni to sit beside him in the great stupa mausoleum which hovers above the assembly. Shakyamuni takes his place next to Many Treasures and then he raises the assembly so everyone can see the two Buddhas. The assembly and the two Buddhas and the leaders of the Bodhisattvas who rise from beneath the ground are the complete Honzon, the object of veneration for observing one's mind. We are gazing at this with the intention of observing our minds and the fundamental truth of our inherent Buddha nature.

2.   Purifying the place of practice: The example for us is found in the Lotus Sutra when the Buddha purifies the land in preparation for the return of his emanations. Numerous times he purifies the land, joins more lands and purifies them and continues to do so until the space is large enough to accommodate the emanations and their retinues.

3.   Ritual accoutrements: This would be your prayer beads (juzu) and your prayer book (kyobon). These are the most common items lay people will have. For priests it would include other items such as a handheld incense burner (egoro); the ritual fan (chukei); flower petal tray (hanazara); handheld bell (inkin); service books, including shomyo; and appropriate priest juzu. These should all be in good repair

and treated respectfully for their importance as skillful means to your practice.

4.   Cleanliness and vestments: For lay practitioners this would mean properly and neatly dressed. I realize that current fashion has ripped jeans as acceptable for many semi-formal public occasions. I would question the wearing of ripped jeans for service, but fundamentally it is your choice. The operating principle should be to dress as if you had an invitation to see the Buddha. I'll let you be the guide as to what that would look like. For priests, it means the proper robe for the occasion, and we have lots of robes for all sorts of occasions, certainly more than the Buddha ever had. It means keeping the kesa clean and maintained. This is the part of the robe that is considered to represent the Buddha's robe. It can be identified by having a patch work appearance. It comes in several sizes though traditionally it is either a 5-panel or 7-panel kesa. There is a special way to wear the robes and kesa when hiking. Also considered the same is the wagesa, which is an abbreviated kesa that derives from the kesa being folded up when riding horses. Some lay practitioners have been given lay wagesa. These should always be worn when performing services. There is a prohibition on eating, drinking, or going to the toilet when wearing either the kesa or wagesa, so keep that in mind.

5.   Offering incense and flowers: These are self-explanatory, but there is something I would like to say. Living in modern cities may make flower offerings challenging. We offer flowers in the same way the gods and heavenly deities rain flowers on the Buddha and those who are attaining enlightenment. They beautify and create a pleasing place for us to attain our enlightenment. It isn't always possible to have fresh flowers. While cut flowers are

ideal, the overarching factor is your heart, your spirit. If you don't have flowers, then you can't offer them. On occasions when you desire to have flowers but have no money or access, consider handmaking a paper flower for the service and then cremating it afterward. Do not reuse. Incense may be problematic for some people either due to health issues, restrictions in their living space or concerns such as safety. Do not burn incense if someone in the house is on oxygen. Pure oxygen is highly flammable, and you can't smell it. Always use common sense. It should be noted that food and fruit offerings are never placed directly on the altar. Use a dish or tray, or at the very least place a mat of paper or fabric under the offering. In temples there are a variety of offering dishes, trays, and stands, each with its own prescribed way of display and arrangement.

From Nichiren Shu

6.   Bells and percussion instruments: Lay practitioners may or may not have some of these items. They are not required, although it would be nice if you have a bell. The size of the bell is unimportant. More important is how you "play" the bell. In Nichiren Shu, we strike the bell not by hitting it directly on the rim, nor by running the striker around the inside rim as one would do with what is called a singing bowl. The proper way to ring the bell is an upward stroke to the rim of the bell. This produces a more pleasing sound. The bell is not a gong. At home you may or may not have a mokusho or mokugyo. The mokusho is a round flat wooden drum that produces a loud, high-pitch sound, depending upon size. The pitch and loudness allow the sound to be heard above the taiko drums used in temples. The mokugyo is fish

shaped, sort of roundish with a slit in between the lips of the mouth. This produces a much softer, deeper sound. The mokugyo is traditionally used during memorial services as it is a more somber sound. Neither the mokusho or mokugyo are necessary for personal practice. In a temple, there are more bells and percussion instruments. I will only speak of a few. There is the inkin, which is a handheld bell used mostly during shomyo to signal to the priests to do certain things, either movements or singing. There is the kei, which is a plank gong. It is used as a signal in various parts of the service. There are also drums such as large taiko or the hand-held Uchiwa Daiko. You may see in some temples the use of nyo and hachi, which are symbols and gongs for the most formal occasions and limited shomyo. There are other items beyond the scope of this book's purpose.

7.   Service Manner: There are many instructions given to priests that dictate virtually every movement, placement of hands and feet, walking, sitting, and rising. Nothing a priest does during a ceremony is without some instruction. At first it is almost overwhelming all the things one must be attentive to. In time it does become more natural. For the lay practitioner, having in your mind the solemn yet joyful activity of honoring the Buddha and his teachings will help you. Always try to sit as erect as possible, whether in a chair, on a cushion or mat, or on the floor. When sitting in a chair avoid slouching. Sit on the edge of the chair, and let your back support itself. For those with skeletal or muscular limitations, use common sense and try your best to sit upright. Having the necessary items arranged in front of you before the service will help you maintain your focus during the service and will allow you to flow smoothly from one part of the ceremony to another. Being discombobulated is to be avoided. I hesitate to use the analogy of a play or

performance, yet in some ways this is a performance of your great delight and appreciation to the Three Jewels – the Eternal Buddha, the Dharma, and the Sangha.

In closing this section, please keep in mind these are skillful means. They are not the object. The tools, guidelines, and procedures have been created to help you prepare your body, mind, spirit, and environment so that you may fully and deeply enter the great teaching of the True Dharma of the Lotus Sutra. Nothing bad happens if you get it wrong or if you are unable to do some of these things. The hope is that doing what you can, which may change over time through the causes you make with what you have, will bring you delight and joy.

What follows does not include the singing of traditional hymns (shomyo). If you know how to properly perform shomyo, then, of course, you may include them in your practice. If you are unfamiliar, or have not been instructed on how to properly perform the hymns, then it is best to omit them. It is important to perform the shomyo correctly so that when you are in a community setting you contribute to the harmony. Each of the hymns has specific movements associated with it, and some of the melodies can be tricky, especially for the Western ear used to a different tonal scale.

1. Invocation - Kanjo

The Invocation is the first spoken portion of the service following the ringing of the bell three times. The Invocation provided in service books is a generic version and you may find your temple uses different words. The Invocation can be personalized for each temple and may include the names of founders, or special protective deities whom the temple revers or are enshrined at the temple. Speak to your minister to see if there is a special Invocation. Also, in some temples only the minister reads the Invocation and in others it may be done in unison. Again, follow your minister's instructions. For your personal practice, however, offer the Invocation when doing a complete service. Our Invocation, just as the meaning of the word implies, is a request, one you make with sincerity and humility. There is, in fact, both a request and a thank you taking place. You are making your request to the Buddha, the founder Nichiren, and important personages and deities, while thanking them for hearing your current request and for their past actions in your support. While not spoken, there is also the understanding that you will uphold the teachings of the Buddha, follow the examples of the Bodhisattvas, and, in all ways, represent the Lotus Sutra favorably. You may not have realized all of that was going on. Now that you do, you can expand your entry into the formalities of the service.

2. Worship – Raihai

There are many ways of bowing before the Buddha. Where the bowing takes place will determine the correct bow to perform. We are exhorted to do this bowing with reverence. It is important to master this correctly, and I encourage you to get full instruction from your teacher or priest. For the purposes of this publication I will only describe in general terms how to do gassho and kikorai, or what is commonly called raihai.

Think of these bows as the physical practice of namu. There is the verbal and or mental namu, which we do with our heart and thoughts. Then there is the physical practice of namu, which we perform by doing gassho and raihai.

Gassho is the placing of the palms of the hand together in front of you. To perform this hand gesture properly, hold your palms together parallel to your body, with the tips of the fingers touching right at the neck line – or for guys at your Adam's apple. Slightly tilt the hands forward with the arms still pressed against the sides of your body. The arms should not be like wings extended away from your body nor should the palms of your hands be any further from your body than allowed by pressing the arms against your sides. The palms are not extended, and the arms are not extended. The head can, if appropriate, be tilted slightly forward, or a deeper tilt may be appropriate to express more reverential deference.

We perform gassho in many instances outside services. People do gassho in greeting or in parting. It can be done in both formal and informal settings. When I worked as a hospital chaplain, I would perform gassho when greeting or parting with peers in the hospital or, if appropriate, to patients and families, especially if I am in robes or acting in an official priestly capacity. Those instances when I am in robes I do gassho even to non-Buddhists, except in the hospital where I may be wearing my robes and yet acting in a non-denominational, or multi-faith capacity.

I do not believe there is any time when doing gassho would be wrong.

For kikorai or, as it is sometimes called, raihai, you are performing a deep prostration that takes you all the way to the floor. I will do this when I meet other Buddhists, especially monastics of the Theravada tradition. I think it is impossible for me to completely describe this bow. I will provide a general idea here, but please go over it with your teacher.

After placing your hands in gassho, you bend your knees and smoothly lower your body to the floor with the knees touching the floor and your fanny resting on your heels. Then bend forward at the waist until your forehead is touching the floor. Place your outstretched hands palm side up on the floor on either side of your head next to your ears. Then slowly lift them up to just above or right at the top edge of your ear. Envision yourself lifting the Buddha's feet above your head.

In raising the Buddha above our head from this deep bow we are imitating what we read in the sutra.

When I do this bow, I go slowly. After I have my hands on the floor palm side up I pause briefly. Then I slowly elevate my hands and pause again. I then lower them back to the floor and pause. Then I stand up. I do the pauses because I wish to be as intentional as I can. The pause helps me hold in my mind the image of lifting the Buddha. Rushing through tends to cultivate a less reverential mind more interested in moving on.

On the second to last morning of Shingyo Dojo, the final 35-day training in Japan before novices become priests, I was given the opportunity to read aloud the rules and vows of students before the head teacher. It is a solemn act and one not everyone gets to perform. There were, after all, 85 of us taking part in Shingyo Dojo. I was not allowed to read the vows in English and so had to practice doing it in Japanese. There was little time to practice this extra activity, and getting the pacing of the words correct was challenging. The leader of my han (group) didn't think I was good enough to do it and at the last moment wasn't going to allow me. I told him that, regardless of my poor Japanese, it was important that a non-Japanese be allowed to do this as Nichiren intended the Lotus Sutra be spread over the entire world.

In the end, I did a terrible job of pronouncing the words. After the service, the head teacher basically said my Japanese sucked, although not in those exact words. Despite that, he said he wanted everyone to notice how I did raihai. He said that he hadn't seen anyone do it so well and properly. My pauses and doing it slowly and deliberately, as opposed to rushing through, impressed him. I know he was probably just finding something good to say after I did such a poor job on my Japanese pronunciation, but I felt good and afterward the other students came to me asking that I demonstrate raihai. So, yes, I am a firm believer in doing this with feeling. It is not some meaningless formality.

In closing this section, I urge you not to simply go off my descriptions of how to perform these movements but have your teacher demonstrate the correct way to perform gassho and raihai, and offer you corrections and adjustments as needed.

3. Extolling the Sutra – Sandan

Extolling and praising the virtues of the sutra is appropriate before and after reciting the sutra. We do this when we recite Verses for Opening the Sutra. This reading praises the sutra, notes its virtues, and highlights that it is enough just to be near the sutra – physically, mentally, and spiritually – to receive its merits. Our association with the sutra, which is profound beyond words, is all that is necessary to be cloaked in its virtues. As the Verses for Opening the Sutra says, "just as perfume is caught by something put nearby," so, too, do we absorb the flavor and scent of the Lotus Sutra by our constant association with this ultimate truth of the Buddha.

The merits of the Lotus Sutra come to us not because we are special. It is the sutra that is special, and we absorb its merits. The merits do not come to us because we are wise. We are all equally ignorant of the fundamental truth of life without the Lotus Sutra. Regardless of our faith or lack of faith, all the merits contained in the Lotus Sutra come to us because of our practice and association with the teaching of the Buddha.

Following our recitation of the sutra, which includes Odaimoku chanting, we may offer Hoto-ge, the concluding verses of Chapter XI, Beholding the Stupa of Treasures. The odd beat associated with Hoto-ge recitation memorializes Nichiren's exile to Izu Penisula. The general recommendation for doing Hotoge is to include it in your services when you are able. Sometimes in the course of life you may not have the time necesssary, I feel it is better to do what you are able with joy and let go of what you are not ab le to do. It's not harmful if you omit it. There is no punishment waiting for you, only merit or no merit.

4. Sutra Reading and Reciting from Memory – Dokuju

When we recite the sutra we should keep in mind five rules for our recitation: 1) Vocal clarity, 2) Phrase-by-phrase clarity, 3) Fluency, 4) Noble-mindedness, and 5) Solemnity and propriety. There are also three cautions: 1) Mindful we are before the gods and Buddhas, 2) Pray to placate even the spirits of darkness, and 3) Pray to move and delight the people.

When we are in community reciting the sutra, it is said we should do so by the ear. For anyone who has either sung in a choir or played a musical instrument in a band you understand the importance of listening to those around you so that your playing or singing is not just in time or in harmony, but it is also appropriately loud or soft. When we recite in community we are instructed to set aside our personal manner of recitation and concentrate on harmonizing with others. In that way we are all able to enjoy the flavor of the Dharma together.

Daily practice is important as this ensures you gain proficiency in correctly pronouncing the words, adjusting your pace of speaking and tonal quality. In all of this seek to find your own natural style when by yourself. You should not force yourself to be overly ostentatious in your manner of service. If you do not naturally have a deep voice, then do not try to force your voice deeper. I will say, however, that daily practice can help improve your range of voice, which will enable you to better harmonize when in a group setting.

It is desirable to have a place to rest your sutra book so it remains open and your hands free. During the service you begin with your hands in gassho. After the third bell you place your hands in shashu just below your belly button. We do shashu by placing the left palm against the back of the right hand and the thumb of the left hand is inserted into crook of your right thumb and index finger. This may sound confusing so ask your teacher to demonstrate this. As the sutra reciting is nearing the end of the passage the bell is rung and at this time you move your hands to gassho until the end of the sutra.

Finally, the rhythm of the sutra chanting should remain constant. It is permissible when reciting the entire sutra to change the pace once in the beginning and twice at the end. Otherwise practice trying to maintain a steady pace. The natural tendency is to speed up on passages one is familiar with and slow down when reciting an unfamiliar passage.

Be aware of this and do your best to keep the same pace throughout.

5. Directing Thoughts - Unzo

"Unzo is deep and contemplative thinking... In dokuju (reading & reciting the sutra), whether chanting in shindoku or kundoku [and English], it is difficult to maintain deep and contemplative thought; during shodai, it is easy to maintain deep and contemplative thought." Raiju-giki[1]

When chanting in non-English, we can become so focused on getting the pronunciation correct that we get distracted. Chanting in English, we can get distracted by pondering what the words mean and trying to assemble a complete understanding. During Odaimoku, or shodai, we can become bored and our mind wander. Doing unzo beforehand helps us maintain our focus and reminds us of our intention. Unless a specific one is given, a suitable unzo is to read Nichiren's instructions. Failing that, you may simply pause to focus your thoughts.

Once you have begun to master the shindoku reading of the sutra you will find it easier to maintain a more deep and contemplative mind, allowing you to have a transcendent experience. This is more difficult when doing it in English, though not impossible. One thing that can help when doing it in English is to follow the pattern of a syllable by syllable rhythm.

---

1. Shutei Hoyo Shiki, page 272

6. Daimoku Chanting - Shodai

Whenever I lead Daimoku chanting (shodai), I preface it with an instruction to chant with great joy and confidence. We should make great effort to avoid chanting in a lazy, gloomy, or distracted manner. The cultivation of one's inner spirit of joy and confidence enhances our Odaimoku and the Odaimoku enhances our inner spirit. Remember the way we chant and the state of our mind are all causes that have a significant impact on our lives and the benefit of the Odaimoku.

The pace of the chanting should be moderate, not too fast nor too slow. It should be comfortable and allow for easy pronunciation of all the seven characters of Na Mu Myo Ho Ren Ge Kyo. Namu takes one single beat and the remaining characters one beat each. The Raiju-giki suggests a minimum of 300 Odaimoku, though personally I am not a fan of the distraction of counting. Even counting one's beads and doing three complete sets of 108 beads is a distraction. My advice is to know yourself and chant until you are full. Over time you will learn to discern when you've chanted enough. Sometimes the number will be very long and other times it may be as short as 300 repetitions.

7. Transfer of Merit - Eko

The Raiju-giki says: "Because the eko is a respectful address, it should be performed with concentration and mindfulness and even more reverence than dokuju [sutra reading] and shodai [Odaimoku chanting]. There should be no confusion, insincerity, and carelessness, or distraction."

The Shutei Hoyo Shiki cautions against overly formal or flowery language. Pleasing and easy to understand language should be used. We should be able to put our hearts into the eko.

For our daily service we have a model transfer of merit provided in the Prayer. You may change the words if you feel a need to offer something special or on special occasions. Generally, though, the Prayer offers a good model for our daily services.

A few months ago, I had breakfast at a restaurant I had not tried before in Syracuse. The place is called Funk-n-Waffles. Since this was a little personal treat, I ordered a large waffle that came with an abundance of bananas, strawberries, blueberries, and raspberries, all topped with powdered sugar. I wasn't sure if all that would be sweet enough, so I added a small amount of syrup to a small portion. With all the fruit on the waffle I was surprised that the syrup was not only unnecessary, but it made it too sweet. The fruit alone was sweet enough, and I am notorious for wanting my breakfast food to be very sweet.

I offer this to illustrate how the transfer of merit should be pleasing yet straightforward. Too much flowery and unnatural language only interferes with the intent. The words used should invite us into the transfer of merit. The words need to be clear as to the intent of wishing to benefit all beings from our efforts as well as repay our debts of gratitude to the Buddha, our founder and the many people in our lives whom we have learned from.

8. Declaring Vows - Hotsugan

The notion of taking vows has generally lost its significance. I say this because it used to be that when one took a vow, especially a religious vow, one did so with an understating that to break such a vow was a serious matter with serious consequences. Today, many people shrug their shoulders as they walk away, ignoring what they swore to do.

A vow is more than a simple promise. It isn't something undertaken only to be followed when convenient or when there is nothing better to do. When we take vows in Buddhism, whether it is vows to uphold our faith, as in jukai, or the Four Great Vows, we are saying directly to the Buddha, "With my whole heart and being, I will do these things."

Each day we should repeat the Four Great Vows as a pledge we make to the Buddha, a pledge we will carry out. We vow to strive with every ounce, every molecule of our life. It is tempting to make excuses or even forget about these vows. That is a serious mistake.

Whether or not these vows are possible is a distraction from our commitment to benefit all living beings. As Bodhisattvas we seek to ensure that everyone passes through the gate to enlightenment before we do. It is as if we are standing at the threshold of enlightenment, holding the gate open to allow all beings to pass through before we enter.

The low probability of completing each of the vows is not an excuse for failing to try. They are only impossible if we do not strive with our whole being to fulfill these great vows. Daily reading of these vows is key to keeping them fresh in your mind. A conscious effort to remember them for even a moment is a worthy goal.

9. The Three Refuges - Sanki

It is by taking refuge in the Three Jewels – the Buddha, the Dharma, and the Sangha – that we can receive their all-encompassing and complete benefit. We do not create this immeasurable benefit. Rather, our practice makes it possible to receive these benefits. We are refugees lost in the wilderness who have wandered lifetime after lifetime looking for shelter and a means to happiness. Finally, we have come upon the sublime place to attain awakening and achieve our heart's true desire. This place is the refuge of the Buddha, the Dharma, and the Sangha.

With little effort we receive immeasurable benefit. This principle is written about in the Mo-Ho Chih-Kuan. Through our assiduous practices we gradually attain enlightenment. Our objective is enlightenment for all beings. When we take refuge, we may initially only be seeking the end to our suffering, hence we have only exerted small effort. As we continue our practice our focus should begin to shift to the desire to enable all people to experience the great joy we have. To cultivate and manifest the desire to save all beings requires greater effort than to merely think only of oneself. The more we engage in the selfless practice for others, the more our own benefit of enlightenment increases.

It would be a mistake to think we will achieve great benefit if we perform the action of spreading Buddhism without the spirit of giving to others. Such a desire for self is a small effort. We need to cultivate the life that realizes the more we give away, the greater the return, and do so pure in spirit. It is truly a difficult thing to do. That is why it is a great effort.

10. Valediction - Buso

At the beginning of our service we traditionally perform a hymn that invites all heavenly beings – the forces throughout the universe that watch over and protect us – to come and receive the gift of our practice of the Lotus Sutra.

To conclude our service, we thank those same entities for joining us and give them a reverent send-off. As we send them away we are aware that they remain with us always, protecting us as we continue to hold in our thoughts and hearts the teaching of the Lotus Sutra and attempt to act according to the teachings contained within.

Hokke Senbo - Reflection and Repentance

While writing a book it is my practice to share the first draft on my blog. I do this to preview the work, and to provide a means for comments. One blog post generated a question of whether Hokke Senbo, the Reflection and Repentance ceremony, could be performed on an individual basis. The short answer is no.

The ceremony, when done correctly, is complicated and requires many items that are not generally found at home. For example, before the ceremony is even begun a large elephant incense burner is placed at the entrance to the hall. As the participants enter the practice space, they step over this elephant burner. Beyond that there are special hand-held incense burners and special incense for each minister. The shomyo (hymms) sung during the ceremony are some of the most complicated and require special movements to be performed as they are sung. The ceremony even in its most brief form is long, taking as much as two, three or more hours. During the recitation of the sutra, which includes many chapters, circumambulations are performed around the Buddha as well as flower petal tossing.

An important aspect of this ritual is that it be done in community with others who are seeking their own reflection and change. Buddhism is not a solitary practice. To think so is to disregard the Sangha as one of the Three Jewels. It is in community that we are supported, cared for, nourished, and protected.

What is possible to do on an individual basis is to dedicate your practice to personal reflection on the ways your actions have been less than skillful. Consider the ways in which your behavior does not mirror your desired actions. Look deep in your life to understand where the disconnection comes from and how you might do better.

Sometimes it isn't enough to simply acknowledge the disconnection. This is especially true when it is something you do repeatedly. At the heart of it there is some unresolved issue hidden from easy observation. In order to effectively change one's life, the questions behind the questions behind the questions need to be discovered and then answered.

During this process of admitting the less-than-skillful actions, exploring the ways in which they may have hurt someone or impacted others or even your well-being is important. This can be painful. While it is true generally that honesty, especially with oneself, is the best policy, it should be done gently. The idea is to engage in a process that moves you from the unskillful to the skillful in a healthy way. It does no good to beat yourself up.

The way in which you choose to perform this practice is a matter of personal choice. The way to properly perform the Hokke Senbo is not subject to personal preferences.

Five Implements of Skillful Means

Not found in the Shutei Hoyo Shiki is a teaching by Chic-i

in his "Essentials for Practicing Calming and Insight Dhyana Meditation." I feel it is important to include it in this book of important matters. These essentials are Zeal, Vigor, Mindfulness, Discernment, and Single-Mindedness.

Zeal – First, a person must possess the desire, the willingness to change something. Without this aspiring to change there is no initial cause for implementation.

Vigor – Next, a person must approach the task with effort, and a willingness to accomplish the task without letting up. Not being afraid to challenge the root causes of which may be the most difficult. Unrelenting adherence to the Six Perfections, the Eightfold Path even when it seems most difficult or most discouraging.

Mindfulness - Generation of a mind that is able to see what is based upon reality and what is based on our interpretation. A mind that is aware that there are noble acts and acts that are to be avoided. Develop a mind that is free from the outflows of impurity. Being awake in the moment and aware.

Discernment - Discrimination of action based on mindfulness. To make critical judgments about what is wise. Assessments of value and achievements against what will be lost or unattainable by acting a certain way. It isn't always a case of clear-cut choices. Sometimes the choice is between two unpleasant courses that one hopes will yield the greatest potential for future better choices.

Single-Mindedness - Achieving a focus that prohibits us from being distracted and side-tracked. Making a single-minded effort to cultivate one's mind so that nothing can interfere with our efforts.

More Books by Rysuho Jeffus:

Lecture on the Lotus Sutra

Lotus Sutra Practice Guide

Daily Lotus

Incarcerated Lotus

The Magic City

The Physician's Good Medicine

Lotus Path

King Wonderful Adornment

Lire du Sutra du Lotus

Cité Magique

Le Bon Remède du Médecin Habile

Roi Ornement-Merveilleux

Connect with Ryusho Jeffus on-line:

Twitter:
@ryusho @myoshoji

Facebook:
https://www.facebook.com/Ryusho

Facebook Author Page:
https://www.facebook.com/revryusho

Blog:
https://www:ryusho.org/blog

Made in the USA
Middletown, DE
28 March 2018